Beautifully BAD Wanda

A TRUE STORY OF WHEN BEING BAD IS GOOD

Beautifully BAD Wanda

KATHI G. STOGNER

MILL CITY PRESS

Mill City Press, Inc.
2301 Lucien Way #415
Maitland, FL 32751
407.339.4217
www.millcitypress.net

Printed in the United States of America.

ISBN-13: 978-1-5456-6147-5

Respectfully and lovingly dedicated
to my dear grandmother, Wanda Konschak Belinsky,
who gave me both her faith and her feistiness. K.S.

TABLE OF CONTENTS

ACKNOWLEDGMENTS

I want to thank my wonderful mother, Dee Belinsky Glander, for being the first person to read and give me feedback on this story. I also want to thank my graduate school friend Ambra Watkins (author of *Escape From Dark Places*) for working diligently with me through the revision and editing process. I am so grateful for her dedication and patience. Further thanks is due to Kelly Gunzenhauser, another graduate school friend, who was willing to read my manuscript. Their expertise and kindness are truly appreciated. My gratitude also goes out to my husband who understood how much I needed and wanted to share my grandmother's story. To my daughters, I say, "Thank you for always supporting your mama's dream!" And thank you God for my grandmother, Wanda Konschak Belinsky, whom you loved unconditionally and provided with the hope and strength that enabled her to survive horrible pain and to blossom with the joyous beauty of life.

Part 1
LIVING ON THE FARM

Chapter 1

A FAR FROM CHARMING, FARMING LIFE

I wait impatiently for the platter of oily chicken to make its way down the gigantic, wooden table to the end where I sit with the other two youngest children in the Konschak family. As usual, I can't resist, so I nonchalantly flick a rather large crumb from my piece of brown bread into the unsuspecting face of my younger brother, Albert. It hits him directly between the eyes before rolling down the bridge of his nose. He shoots me his customary look of *when I get my hands on you, I'm going to rip that smile off your face* and commences with the slathering of his boiled potatoes in butter. Not pleased with his lack of effort, I proceed in my feeble attempt to further annoy him by standing up and grabbing the satiated platter of sliced tomatoes before he can get any. The chilling voice of my father breaks my concentration like a gunshot in the middle of a quiet night. "Schlechta Wanda! Sit down!" I grumpily sit but not before imagining myself defiantly sticking out my tongue.

Schlechta Wanda. How many times have I heard those words? Hundreds? Thousands? No wonder I am bad. It seems like a self-fulfilling prophecy with me working tirelessly to live up to my father's depiction of me as *Bad Wanda*. Father often speaks in German, especially when he is angry. It is the language he and my mother brought with them from Lodz, Germany, through Ellis Island when first settling in America. *Schlecht* means *bad* in English, and my malevolently poetic father added the *a* at the end so that it would rhyme with Wanda. With God as my witness, very few days go by when I don't hear this burdensome nickname hurled at me in varying degrees of displeasure and spite. After hearing it, I sometimes try to console myself by thinking about new words I've learned from my heavy *Webster's Unabridged Dictionary*. I received it from my second grade teacher years ago, and since I am sneaky, I'm usually able to read it daily. I wish Father would call me any other word found inside that dictionary, anything other than *bad*.

The now almost empty platter of chicken finally reaches me, and I proceed to remove one no longer steaming chicken wing and two of the three remaining neck bones. The neck bones actually contain the sweetest meat, so I don't mind one bit that they are sometimes the only thing left once the mammoth-sized plate reaches my confine of the table. Father sits in his oversized, wooden chair at the head of our gathering like a judge in a courtroom. Mother sits at his left and Grandmother, his mother, at his right. From there, we kids spread out from oldest to youngest, which is why Albert, Martha, and I are at the end.

I can feel the hot grease dripping down my chin as I nibble along the tasty chicken bone, but I don't stop to wipe it. After having already picked multiple bushels of tomatoes in the blazing heat and carrying all of them to the wagon and then into the storage shed near the main barn, I am famished by the time we sit down for our 12:00 p.m. supper. As everyone growing up on a farm knows, you have a filling but not fancy breakfast followed by a huge supper in the afternoon and a smaller dinner in the evening. Supper is undoubtedly my favorite meal of the day, and I am going to thoroughly enjoy it!

A typical day on our 220-acre farm in Hartley, Delaware, consists of me and my nine siblings reluctantly rising at 4:30 a.m. to milk the cows and to gather the countless eggs from the odoriferous hen houses before coming in to devour our breakfast. I milk three of our cows every morning and every night and am mercilessly pecked by ungrateful chickens while I hurry to do my chores. Most of the eggs that I collect will be sold. This means that they need to be cleaned; weighed to designate whether they are small, medium, or large; and packed into crates. It takes thirty dozen eggs to make up one crate. Having to fill up crates every day is a dreary chore that I vehemently despise. There is also the regular task of chopping off the heads of the unlucky chickens selected for personal consumption and sale. Since I have done all of this from the time I was six years old, now that I am double digits, I already feel like if I never lay eyes on another chicken or its eggs that will suit me just fine. I will always believe that one of the worst jobs is cleaning filthy hen houses. That is because the worst smell in the world is the stench of broiling chicken poop on a flaming summer day.

The long, laborious days are also filled up with working in the fields. We do our farm work from early morning until it is done, making for many late nights. When asked, we kids say that we work from morning till done, like *done* is a real time of the day. For us, it is. Oftentimes (and I feel strangely guilty saying this) *done* is the best part of my day because life . . . well, it's all just a lot of work! Depending on the season, we are either planting corn, wheat, hay, strawberries, and tomatoes or picking tomatoes, strawberries, and grapes. Then comes the harvesting and the threshing of wheat and hay along with the cutting and husking of all the corn. I am also the lucky one who gets the time-consuming task of canning blood-red tomatoes and freshly picked green beans in between making salty, delicious pickles.

I stand tall for my age and am long and lean but not skinny. My shoulders are broad and my muscles defined by years of physically demanding labor. I have wavy, dark brown almost black hair. My eyes are such a dark shade of brown that they sometimes appear black. I have long, black eyelashes and fair skin that would be milky white except for all of the hours that I have to spend working outdoors. I become brown like a chestnut anywhere on my body that isn't covered, especially in the summer. One thing that I have never liked about myself is my nose. It's not too big exactly, especially for my very round face and high forehead, but it's not the tiny, cute, pixie nose that some girls possess and I covet. I can say, though, that I have beautiful skin, no big pores or blemishes. I inherited this from my mother with her noticeably lovely and smooth, wrinkle-free complexion. My lips are thin, especially my top lip, so that if I'm not smiling, I look pensive. My personality fits my looks. I am a living oxymoron because those who negatively focus on my flaws see me as mischievous, ornery, stubborn, demanding, and competitive; whereas, favorable people find me to be energetic, tough, determined, bright, generous, and thoughtful. In all honesty, I suppose that all of these words could truly describe me, Wanda Konschak, born January 16, 1916, in Marydel, Delaware. If you were to ask my mother, she would say that I am "feisty yet caring." My father, on the other hand, would sum me up with one word. *Schlecht*. If you consider someone to be a bad person because she won't stay quiet and submissive in the face of injustice and perceived wrong, then I am Schlechta Wanda to you too!

My dear, hard-working mother is always up even before us kids to begin the baking, cooking, cleaning, sewing, fixing, and creative problem solving that lovingly raising a large family on a sizable farm entails. My mother can be strict, but she is always still kind and loving towards us. Father, though, is the ultimate definition of stern. He is extremely harsh and insists that things always be done in a very specific way—*HIS* way. Father dictates what work we do on the farm, and my perception is that he never saves much, if any, work for himself. One thing that my father actually does do is the planting of our corn in rows. The corn is planted in rows that Father demands be perfectly straight. He whines with vexation that no one can get the rows straight except for him, so he is *forced to do it* himself. Poor Father!

I can only recall two specific things that my father actually taught me how to do. They are how to make tasty noodles and how to clean and scrape the obese pigs that are killed in the winter. Making noodles is rather easy and just requires patience, but hog butchering is a dirty, difficult job. Killing then cleaning the pigs and scraping the stiff bristles off of their skin equates to a bloody, smelly mess. The nasty head meat has to be put into tremendous, wash-type pans and cooked. I always find the resulting smell to be absolutely revolting. Blood pudding, liver pudding, and scrapple are all made from this head meat that I can never quite bring myself to eat. Whenever I look at the contents of the pigs' heads, I have flashbacks of their satisfied faces devouring the cabbages and other slop that I've dumped into their pens, and I just can't consume it. I will, however, eat the hams and other cuts of meat that I bring into our smokehouse, and when he helps me, Father is truly talented at making delicious sausages with just the right amount of spice.

People talk about how Father is a good provider, but I have to say that his unloving nature makes me reject that. Father, like the rest of us, will be up early in the morning, but he conveniently disappears for hours at a time. He takes multiple naps daily just like an infant, although he is a grown man. Most of these naps are on the black leather couch in the kitchen after he's had his post-supper beer or beers. He will literally lie for the exact same amount of time on his left side, then his back, and lastly, on his right side. It is his very annoying, daily ritual. We will also sometimes find him asleep in one of the barns or in another of the farm buildings. There are other times when one of us kids will hear obnoxious snoring coming from under a tree or behind a hay bale, and there is never any doubt about who is sleeping so soundly. Father usually appears again at meal times or later in the day to stumble around screaming at us about what we still need to get accomplished before we are *done*, how worthless we are, and how much money we are costing him. We all know he is a liar. All of my brothers and sisters and I firmly believe that he doesn't work as hard on the farm as he makes us work, and for that, we hate him. As the years crawl on, I am actually happy that his drinking is getting heavier and worse. Surprised? Don't be. When I don't do things *HIS* way, it becomes easier and easier to outrun his belt.

Chapter 2
THE KONSCHAK CLAN

My family consists of my father Johann (John) Konschak, my mother Pauline Zarbok Konschak, my grandmother Theresa Konschak, and eleven children. From oldest to youngest we are Gustov (Gus), John Jr. (Johnny), Otto, Julia (Jule), William (Bill), Emma, Paula, Richard, Wanda, Albert Max, and Martha Helen. My father's mother, Theresa, was born on April 18, 1837, in Germany and married Aldoph Konschak. In 1875, they moved from the southern part of Germany to Lodz, which is in present day Poland but was then Russia. In Lodz, the family tried various ways of making a living including operating a gristmill and an inn and slaughtering animals to sell their meat. My father, the youngest son in his very large family, was born in Lodz on July 27, 1877. He later helped to support his family by working long, tedious hours as a weaver in a textile factory. All the Germans lived in one area of Lodz and had their own Lutheran church. The Konschaks were always highly involved in all aspects of the church, which even included schooling because the church pastor was also the teacher of the children in the area.

Tiny but strong, Grandmother Theresa birthed fifteen children. Since my father was her baby, she always spoiled him rotten. Theresa came to America in 1904 from Lodz. Once my parents were established on their first farm in Marydel, Delaware, she came to live with them for most of the year. In the winter, Grandmother lives in Philadelphia with her daughter, Frances Hantwerker. In the spring and summer, she comes to live with us on the farm for a minimum of six long months that always seem to last for an eternity. I know from the 1910 United States Census that twelve of her children are still alive, so I don't think it's fair that the rest of them don't have to put up with her. Whether completely justified or not, I don't really like my grandmother. She's not particularly nice to me, and I'm consistently angry at her because of the harsh and vindictive way she treats my mother. It's also extremely difficult not to blame Grandmother for the death of my brother Otto.

My mother, Pauline, was born on January 30, 1881, in Olikof, Poland, to Theodore Zarbok. The Zarbok family originally came from the Ruhr Valley coal region of Germany. I can tell that Mother dearly loved her siblings because she named me, Paula, Gus, and Otto after her own brothers and sisters. She often tells Martha and I stories about her brother, Otto, who was tragically killed in a German coal mine. Mother comments that our brother, Otto, had the same pudgy cheeks, dark eyes, and fly-away hair that refused to stay slicked down that her own brother had possessed before his untimely death.

Mother says that she always wanted to marry a smart, hard-working, Lutheran man, which is why she married my father on June 6, 1900, in the Church of Saint Joseph in Lodz. Pastor Titrich performed the ceremony while my father's friend Ewald Guze skillfully played the accordion and his daughter, Olga Guze, sang. Little did my mother know that her diligent, religious man would become a lazy, abusive, heavy drinker who cares more about having money then about the well-being of his own family. I hope that if the day ever comes when she fully understands this fact, she will still have enough time to save herself. My mother truly does love Father with a profound kind of unconditional love that I cannot understand. Maybe she loves a part of him that us kids never get to see, or she only remembers the courageous and skilled things that he's accomplished. Either way, I cannot fathom her love for, nor her loyalty to, my father.

Back in the time that my parents lived in Lodz, there was a law that every young man had to serve in the army. Before entering, each person had a thorough medical examination. My father had absolutely no desire to go into the military. Some may call it wisdom, while others may call it cowardice, but Father was determined not to join. He has a way of raising up his right arm until it makes a horrible, loud cracking noise like bone grinding against bone. It causes a shudder to run up anyone's spine who hears it. He did this trick at his medical exam, quickly raising up his arm and making it crack like heck. It made him appear disabled and got him dismissed and out of serving his time. Perhaps worried that he might again be called on, Father hastened his plans to leave for America. He was only able to do so because his own father had generously left enough money in trust to get him, his wife, and their two baby sons to "the land of the free and the home of the brave." It was truly a life-changing gift. My cynical side wonders if on his deathbed my grandfather felt compelled to compensate my father for some abuse or horror he had suffered at his hands. It would help explain Father's cruelty to us, if my grandfather was terrible to him. A much more altruistic and commonly held view is that Grandfather Konschak truly loved my father and wanted to bless him with the gift of a new life in America.

Mother says she and Father quickly left Lodz and traveled to Hamburg, Germany, in 1903. At the Hamburg port, they boarded the *Pretoria* with my brothers Gus and Johnny and headed to America. My father had family members who already lived in Delaware, New Jersey, and Pennsylvania. They had written to him about glorious opportunities in the United States of America. In fact, most of my father's family had already settled in America. They found it to be a place of greater opportunities to make a better life for themselves and their families. Mother, though, had to leave her entire birth family behind when she heroically ventured to America with her husband.

Like many before them, my parents decided to risk everything and to leave all that they knew behind in their native land of Germany in order to come to the United States. There were other relatives who traveled to America at the same time as my parents. They included Father's widowed brother Frank, Frank's three-year-old son named Oscar, and Father's sister and brother-in-law (Frances and Andreas Hantwerker) and their children.

I understand that overcrowding on the boat was definitely a vexatious issue, but the main torment was the dreadful seasickness. According to my mother, nearly everyone on board the *Pretoria* was deathly seasick, and she had never before seen so many people so terribly sick all at the same time. Mother says that the smell of stale vomit permeated the air making it difficult to breath. The stench often created a chain reaction of vomiting that was nearly impossible to escape. I imagine she felt like an overworked nurse trapped in a stagnant, airless hospital wing surrounded by sickly patients who couldn't stop throwing up on her. I can only fathom the extreme difficulty my mother, who was six months pregnant, must have had entertaining and caring for her two young children under such conditions. The seemingly endless boat trip took six weeks on rough and dangerous waters. They finally arrived thankfully, eagerly, yet fearfully in the Port of New York on July 24, 1903. For some unknown reason, they didn't have to go through the Ellis Island immigration center, which saved them a lot of time. Father's sister, Aunt Frances, decided that her family would live in Delaware to have more space for all of her children even though Father's oldest brother, Julius, was already settled in Millville, New Jersey, with his large family. My parents decided that New Jersey was the best initial choice for them and chose to begin their American life in Millville near my Uncle Julius.

Less than three months after arriving in America, my dear brother Otto was born on October 5, 1903. After a short time in Millville, my parents moved the growing family to Philadelphia in order to find work. Julia and William were both born in Philadelphia while my parents worked, scrimped, and saved up enough money to purchase a small farm of their own. In early 1907, they purchased their first American farm in Marydel, Delaware, about a mile from the Maryland border. The farm there had plentiful apple trees and a large, one-acre garden that we used to grow our own food. The house had four bedrooms upstairs and three rooms downstairs but no plumbing. My father continued to work in Philadelphia while Mother and my older brothers worked the land. Mother says that it was the only way that they could survive.

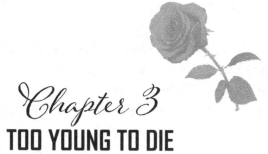

Chapter 3
TOO YOUNG TO DIE

I believe that it was sometime in 1907 that my brother Otto was tragically killed in the kitchen of our farmhouse. None of the adults like to discuss it, but from what I gather from my mother, young Otto was scalded to death by hot water that had been left in an area of the kitchen where he frequently played. The specifics are that Grandmother Theresa placed a large pot of recently boiling water on a wooden, kitchen bench. Jule and Otto were noisily running around the kitchen playing together, as they often did, so why my grandmother ever decided to do such an irresponsible thing is truly baffling. I can't imagine that she would have purposely wanted to kill Jule or Otto because even the most angry, vengeful human would have to be a fiend to kill a child. It had to have been an accident. It had to have been a dreadful mistake that she surely must have felt remorseful about for the rest of her life.

At some point that terrible morning, Otto and Jule were behind the wood stove happily playing underneath the long, narrow bench. Grandmother drank coffee all day long and would just throw an entire small burlap bag full of coffee beans into a boiling pot. Instead of leaving the pot on the side of the stove like she normally did, my grandmother moved it to the bench. Otto accidentally rammed into the bench, turning the entire bucket of scalding water over on top of himself and Jule. Jule was also burned but not nearly as horribly as Otto. He was brutally scalded from his head to his little feet. Since the pot was tall and wide and had been up on the bench, there was virtually no part of my poor brother that was not covered by the hellishly hot water when it fell. I cannot comprehend the pain he must have endured as his skin melted away exposing raw nerves to the open air. There was really nothing they could do to help him in his suffering. Gus told me that when Mother tried to remove Otto's shirt to release some of the heat from his body, several layers of flesh peeled off of his arm. I can only hope and pray to God that Otto went into shock and didn't actually feel anything after the first few minutes of unfathomable agony. Gus says Otto never made a sound, but John Jr. says that he remembers him frantically screaming, crying, and moaning. Please God, let John Jr.'s memories be incorrect.

I don't know how long Otto lived after being so badly scalded, but it wasn't long. I think that he was about four, but I don't know the exact date of his catastrophic death. Otto was not listed with the rest of the family on the Delaware Census for 1910, proving that he was already dead. I do know with utter certainty that Mother never left his side while he lay dying and that she undoubtedly attempted to sooth him with her earnest prayers and motherly utterances. Otto was buried in an unmarked grave in Thomas's Chapel located near Marydel. I figure stingy Father decided it was too costly to purchase a tombstone and have it engraved with the name *Otto Konschak*. It was left for those who loved Otto to engrave his memory on their hearts. In the case of some, like me, who never even had a chance to meet him, we had to engrave his essence and image in our minds and on our souls with the help of Mother's many stories and cherished memories. Emma, Pauline, Richard, Albert, and I were all born in Marydel after Otto died, but we kept him alive inside of us and loved him as if he were still present. Oddly, even Martha, who wasn't born until 1920, talked about our brother Otto as if he was one of her favorite playmates. I also often saw her staring at him in a family photograph that was taken in 1906. That black and white picture showing two or three-year-old, little Otto proved to Martha that he was real even though she never got to see him in person. There he stood next to Gus and in front of Father who was seated in a chair. Beautiful Mother sat in the center of the picture holding baby Jule in her lap. John Jr. stood to Mother's right with his hand gently placed on her knee. Grandmother Theresa sat in a high-backed wicker chair on the far left and appeared to be using both of her hands to forcibly hold John's right arm on her lap. The most important thing about the photograph was that Otto was in it. It was the only professional family picture that my parents ever had made. They had no idea that Otto would die soon after it was taken, but an omniscient God knew. I firmly believe that God put it on their hearts to have that portrait taken because it would later bring my mother some peace and moments of joy every time she looked at her beloved baby boy in it. Dear little Otto, such a precious child whose life on Earth was much too short.

Chapter 4

THE GOOD AND BAD OF CHASING THE AMERICAN DREAM

The Konschak family, the Hantwerker family, and several other Lutheran families who settled in the Marydel-Hartly area formed a church group in 1910. Pastor Franke, from Philadelphia, was the first to serve as minister, followed by Pastor Ohlinger, who traveled a tremendous distance roughly once a month to lead the service. Pastor C.T. Ohlinger of New York had been called by the Lutheran Church-Missouri Synod to the position of missionary-at-large to serve Delaware and the Eastern shore of Maryland in 1913. Sometimes Pastor Totzke would be able to lead the service when Pastor Ohlinger couldn't attend because of his travels. At that time, the church services were held in members' homes. Church and Sunday school were mainly held at the home of William Rohmann in Henderson, Maryland, but soon the services were regularly conducted at our home because my parents owned an organ. Pastor Ohlinger played the organ so that hymns could be sung more easily. The ministers would often opt to stay overnight with us because "the Konschak family is so hospitable." I know our food was delicious and our beds warm thanks to my mother, and apparently, my father was an interested listener and knowledgeable conversationalist when a minister was around. If no preacher was available, my father would conduct the service himself. He always did see a need for us to have religious training and community worship, for which I am truly grateful. My mother loved church as well and especially enjoyed loudly singing all of the hymns even though she had no vocal training. I followed in her footsteps, belting out the songs with exuberance and joy even though I often got dirty looks from Albert who said I sang off key.

The church situation changed in 1918, soon after Albert was born, because my father bought a substantially larger 220-acre farm about three-and-a-half miles from our farm in Marydel. The new, bigger farm was in Hartly, Delaware, and consisted of an old house, a barn, and a grainery. But here too, there were not enough buildings to house all the cows, horses, and family; so, with the son of some German friends, Father first built an even more immense house. My father always was an extremely talented and masterful builder. We lived in the old house while the more spacious, new home was being built. The new house had five large bedrooms and a colossal living room, dining room, and kitchen. In the back of the house, Father and his German friends also built an egg room for washing the eggs with wet rags before putting them into egg crates. In the front of the new house, they built a very long porch. Paula told me that it rained a great deal during that summer that Father built the new home. The rain hampered his plans and kept him constantly wet and irritable; whereas, all of us kids often went swimming in the muddy ditches and thought it was wonderful. I was only about three, so I don't remember this, but I have to admit that it brings a smile to my face to think that something that gave his children much joy also caused my father tremendous consternation.

Once the additional house was completed, the old one was converted into a cow barn with a silo. My father and his friends also built a horse barn with a hay loft on top followed by another immense barn with a hay loft because when it comes to barns, one can never have enough. The second floor of the barn was used for grain, wheat, and corn, while the first floor was used for everything else. Father next wanted to add multiple chicken houses (also called chicken stables) that were similar to those of the seven other German chicken farmers who lived all around us. The chicken houses were eighteen feet wide by sixty feet long, and all the farmers helped each other with these as well as with any other type of building that needed to be constructed. The chicken stables had warm nests consisting of individual, small wooden crates filled with straw and stacked one on top of the other. These nests covered one whole wall and ran the sixty foot length of the building, while the roosts covered the wall on the other side. The roosts resembled shelves and started about two feet off the ground. They were staggered and placed one foot above each other until they reached the ceiling. It was necessary to stagger the roosts in order to keep the occupying chickens from pooping on the chickens below them. This made for a total of about six rungs running the entire length of each stable. We kids had to clean the nasty chicken stables and put in all fresh straw once a week. Trust me when I say you haven't smelled bad until you've breathed in the stench of a hot chicken stable after a week of steady chicken poop. The odor was almost unbearable.

After finishing the building of the house, barns, and stables, my father and his friend's son started to improve on the fencing of our fields for cow pasture and on bettering the soil for planting. My older siblings were sometimes allowed to go to school, which left us young children to watch the cows and to make sure that they didn't escape while the fencing was being built or repaired. Richard said that I was often made to be outside monitoring cows, and that he frequently spotted me sprinting back to the house screaming, "Snake! Snake!" with ear piercing voracity. This might explain many of my childhood nightmares that frequently involved terrifying snakes of enormous size.

My youngest sibling, Martha, was born with the help of a midwife at the Hartly home in 1920 and was my parents' eleventh and last child. Just as the Konschak family grew, so did the farm. Today, there are nineteen buildings, and the majority of them are lengthy chicken houses with large runs. The fact is that as time passes, our farm continues to become more and more of a chicken farm. Father started out buying 3,000 fluffy chicks every spring, and now it's 5,000. We have special, long stoves in different sections of the chicken houses with something like little rooms for every 500 chickens. These stoves keep our plethora of chicks toasty and contented. When they are three months old, the unlucky roosters will be taken out and sold for spring fryers, and a minimum of 1,500 chickens will be raised to produce eggs. We kids used to gather around 1,000 eggs by hand each and every day until Father purchased the 5,000 chicks in the spring, nearly doubling our workload, but he doesn't care one bit. After the chickens, our cows are the second largest group of animals on the farm, followed by horses and pigs. The gigantic work horses used to be especially important for the pulling of our farm equipment, but now more and more of that equipment is becoming mechanized. We keep them nonetheless. We also have several horses just for riding that we try to sneak off and enjoy whenever Father isn't paying attention.

I also really savor stealing any rare, spare moments to take off my shoes and walk barefoot through the soft, tickling grass or to climb up into a sprawling tree or one of the warm barn lofts. I love staring at the tremendous oak and maple trees that spot the landscape around our farmhouse. Colorful flowers, herbs, and garden plants also speckle the property closest to the house. My favorites are Mother's stunning roses. Their colors and fragrance are otherworldly. In that sense, the beauty of nature's colors, textures, and scents is always around me; unfortunately, that magnificence is often lost in the daily, sweaty toil of a life of servitude lived on a farm ruled by a stoic father.

With all of our animals and so much land that is always planted with corn, wheat, strawberries, tomatoes, cabbage, and hay and a tremendous vegetable garden filled with edibles for our large family, we appear to have it made on the Konschak farm. To all his neighbors and friends, my father is a successful farmer and a successful father. Neither one of these concepts is ever verbalized by any of his children. It is every child on the farm who keeps it running and profitable. Notice that I say *child* because it seems to me like Father spends more and more of his time passed out in one of the barns, the shed, or under a tree in the orchard.

I know that John Konschak has a reputation for being a hard worker. I understand that when he and Mother first came to America, he worked long hours in sweat inducing factories in Philadelphia. He had to have toiled incessant hours to save enough for the small farm that was later sold in order to purchase the large farm where we now live. I know that for many years, he continued to labor and to earn money in the city during the week while leaving Mother to run the entire farm on her own with my siblings. It is clear that Father had to have strained, sacrificed, and suffered for the prosperity he now hoards and never lets us enjoy. But as I mentioned before, my sisters and brothers and I do not often witness his work ethic. We all hold strong resentment towards him for the way he works us like dumb animals while he conveniently disappears for numerous hours every day. If only he would be kind while he uses us, maybe we could put on blinders and not grow bitter.

When I was a very little girl in the early 1920s, we Konschaks started attending church in Rising Sun, Delaware, near Dover, Delaware. William told me that when we first started going to church in Rising Sun, we rode a two-horse buggy with two seats and took feed for the horses to eat while the family was in the service. The mission pastor eventually merged the Rising Sun and the Marydel-Hartly groups together to form Saint John's Evangelical Lutheran Church in Dover on December 23, 1923. The congregation members were not only German but also Polish, Russian, Czechoslovakian, Dutch, Swiss, and English. My father was one of the original founders of Saint John and was very influential in both securing the land and in the building of the church. The church building was finally finished and ready for dedication on May 5, 1925. I am very proud of Father for all of that, although I have never told him so.

Church is a major component of the Konschak life, and I love it. It is one thing that I can readily thank my father for giving me. We put on our nicer clothes, and I help my sisters fix their hair to look particularly lovely and stylish. John Jr. is a saint because he always stays home on Sundays so that the rest of the family can go to Sunday school and church. Farming families never get to take vacations. Even short excursions, like attending church, require someone willing to stay on the farm the entire time.

Father loads the horse-drawn wagon up with our family and off we go from Hartly to Dover for church. My favorite part is learning about how I am saved by grace and not by my good works because, as you will see, I keep the name Schlechta

Wanda for legitimate reasons. Church provides me with peace. It is there that I come to understand that inevitably failing in my attempts to be good and do good don't damn me to hell, because Jesus took my punishment on the cross. Wow! It is a relief even greater than when Father is unable to catch me, and I escape his dreaded, leather belt with its heinous metal buckle. I know that a central focus of my life will always be church and my church family because of the help and hope God gives me there. If God can look through "Jesus lenses" and see me as beautiful instead of bad, I wonder if maybe one day my father can too. Church and my faith in Jesus are honestly two of the main things that get me through this life that is often brutal and exhausting. Along with my siblings and my mother, these things keep me alive.

Chapter 5

WHY COULDN'T I HAVE BEEN A DUMB CAT?

I remember one particular summer day that pretty well summarizes my existence. I rose before 4:30 a.m. and went to collect eggs from our never-ending chicken houses. I walked the seemingly infinite lines of hen boxes gathering the oval eggs while trying to avoid being mercilessly pecked or scratched. Then, after breakfast, it was straight to the fields to gather ripe, red tomatoes. I enjoyed the cool mist that still hung in the air and clung to my meticulously fixed hair as I traversed the dirt road leading to the back fields of our property. The tomatoes were plump and crimson, almost oozing over with juicy deliciousness as I began the drudgery of picking them. The tiny hairs on the stems and leaves of the tomato plants have always made me itch, but I inevitably have to touch them in order to extract the ripe fruit. That day was no different, and the skin on my hands and arms immediately turned red. It wasn't so bad at the beginning while the air was still crisp and the humdrums had not yet set in. I grabbed multiple tomatoes at one time, lowering them into the white cotton satchel that hung over my neck and one of my shoulders. Mother had made the satchels for us to make it quicker and easier to pick the tomatoes and to deliver them to the bushel baskets at the end of the rows. The knapsacks also enabled us to avoid contending with the surprisingly heavy baskets until they were completely full, and therefore, needed to be carried to the wagon and eventually the shed. Without the sacks, we would have been forced to drag each bushel along, and every few steps would have become more and more difficult as the basket became heavier and heavier.

I was able to amuse myself for a little while by singing some of my favorite church songs. "Amazing Grace, Onward Christian Soldiers, and The Old Rugged Cross" were welcome distractions as I belted them out; unfortunately, this self-entertainment was short lived. My focus shifted quickly to how much I wanted to be done with this damn chore. I also thought about how badly I wanted to fill as many baskets as my older siblings while also managing to have more than Albert, which, by the way, I usually did. Soon my neck and shoulder began to ache terribly as I tried to stuff more and more tomatoes into my satchel. More in the bag, meant fewer trips to the end of the row. The permanent indentation in said shoulder began to throb painfully, and there was no end to the hurt in sight.

By 11:00 a.m., the unrelenting heat of the sun had me sweating profusely and opting to throw my large-brim, straw hat to the ground in order to allow more heat to escape from my wet, dark locks and stifled head. I knew that the result would be terrible sunburn, but I didn't care. I could only focus on that moment, and I was too hot, too tired, and too thirsty to be heedful. "My kingdom for a glass of water!" I yelled out to no one in particular. My salty smell soon attracted flies, which began to buzz around me attempting to land. They irritated me enough to cause me not to notice that my right foot was quickly becoming engulfed by red ants angered by my carelessness in stepping directly on their anthill. The sharp stings of their bites alerted me, and I quickly removed my foot from their home and stamped around heavily trying to knock them off. Of course, I had on my high lace-up shoes which weren't easily removed. I worked frantically to loosen the tie from its various metal loops and ended up with several painful ant bites on my hands as well. "Dammit! Dammit!" I screamed, even though I knew that I shouldn't be cursing. At least I wasn't using the Lord's name in vain like I sometimes heard adults doing.

"I hate this!" I yelled loudly, fully acknowledging that I still had to carry all my heavily loaded tomato baskets to the shed before supper and would have to come back out here afterwards to pick for several more hours before dinner. The monotony of it all was so oppressive. I wanted to be reading a classic, doing arithmetic problems, or conducting a science experiment. I did not want to spend eight hours of my day picking tomatoes! How sad that the high point of the day would be my practiced ability to brag about how many bushels of tomatoes I had picked. This would be topped off by milking my three cows, feeding the chickens, bringing them fresh water, and cleaning up their nasty poop. I kept in mind that chickens are substantially worse than cows or pigs when it comes to both cleanliness and aroma, and that didn't brighten my sagging spirits. I knew that even after dealing with my assigned animals, I would still have to finish off my house chores before literally falling into bed. All of this would then finally be over. But wait! In only a few hours, I'd have to get up and do it all again and again and again—seemingly into infinity.

What big adventures lay in store for me? None! What challenging of my mental talents? None! What did I have to look forward to? NOTHING!!! At least that is how I felt on that fly and ant infested, hellishly hot, drudgery laden, creativity lacking, boredom inspiring, summer day on the Konschak farm. To top it all off, by the time I lugged my last container of tomatoes into the shed, I had a terrible headache from squinting into the severe August sun. As I walked past our main barn on my way to the house, a lazy barn cat mocked me by silently emerging to carelessly lick her white paws. She had clearly just been napping because she stretched several times before commencing with the cleaning of her feet and then moved on to her onyx ears. I tiredly shuffled over and looked down with an irritated expression on my face. The pampered cat then proceeded to look up at me flippantly with a countenance of relaxed expectation. Did she really think that I was going to pet her? "Dumb cat!" I screamed as I stormed petulantly past her. I was completely unwilling to admit that I was jealous of a feline. I chose denial instead of truth and attempted to console myself by imagining that I too was free and contented. In hindsight, it is completely obvious that I was indeed intently envious of a cat that day. But who could blame me? Really. Who could?

Chapter 6
ODE TO PAULA

For as long as I can remember, my older sister Paula has been getting out of farm work. She often stays in bed until 9:00 a.m. and then comes out to the fields when the rest of us are already halfway done with our work. Even after getting to sleep in, Paula still acts sickly. She often has, or supposedly has, a debilitating headache accompanied by fatigue and weakness. Just the other day, I heard one of my siblings ask, "Where's Paula?"

"She can't work in the fields picking tomatoes today because she might faint," stated Mother.

Another time, Martha complained that Paula hadn't shown up to milk her cows resulting in Martha having to milk twice as many.

"She didn't come to help me collect all the eggs from the hen house either," I added.

"Paula will be resting in her room today until around 10 because she is feeling very ill," Mother interjected, and that was that.

Paula has never had any major illnesses or diseases and has never been severely injured. What exactly is wrong with her? We children don't know and have vindictively come to the conclusion that she is a lazy and talented faker. Whether or not she is truly sickly and physically weaker than the rest of us or simply a gifted actress, I suppose we'll never know for sure. The only one who knows the absolute truth is Paula, and she's sticking to her original story.

From the time I was nine years old, Mother had me washing down the entire enormously elongated, front porch while perched precariously on a ladder. When I asked why Paula didn't have to assist me, Mother replied, "You do it better than Paula. You do it better than anybody else." Well, when you get praised for something, you feel like a big thing. I felt appreciated, valued, and like I'd really done something special. I told myself that I actually was better at cleaning than anyone else in my family, and my perfectionist personality wouldn't let me miss even a single spec of dirt after that. I cleaned like I did everything else—as if my life depended on it, and at times, maybe it did. I have always been perpetually driven to excellence and sometimes have to do things in a specific way, even sometimes in a definite order. Maybe I'm just extremely hard-working? I don't know, but after a while, the glitz of doing things "better than anybody else" has lost its appeal; still, I continue my same work ethic. You know, sometimes it really stinks to be good at something, particularly when people use it to their advantage and to your detriment!

One humid noon when I was about eleven, I clearly remember shuffling my fatigued and sweaty body towards the house to eat supper. I looked up and saw Paula idly peeking out of her second-story bedroom window. Her pale, sweat-free face was barely recognizable behind the white, lace curtains, and it was just too much for me to stand. I had already had a long, exhausting morning filled with the heavy, grinding work of picking tomatoes while Paula had lollygagged around in her room. Would she have to come outside and help me after we ate supper, or would she get to stay in the room all day? Unable to stop myself, I stared up at her and began singing, "More rain, more rest, Paula shits in the chicken's nest! More rain, more rest, Paula shits in the chicken's nest!" Soon Albert, Martha, and Richard joined me in the serenade of our "sickly" sister. "More rain, more rest, Paula shits in the chicken's nest," we bellowed. It wasn't long before I could barely get out the words as I strained to keep myself from laughing hysterically at my ingenuity. I had taken an old, well-known nursery rhyme and inserted an ending that amply summed up my feelings regarding Paula's perceived lack of work habits. My song even incorporated our infamous chickens, their nests, and their poop. Poor Paula's face quickly disappeared from the window as she ducked down to avoid eye contact. I felt a bit guilty, but that didn't keep me or the others from continuing our catchy chant all the way to the front door. From that day forward, my "Ode to Paula," as I like to call it, has become a familiar mantra for us kids as we sometimes light-heartedly and sometimes resentfully (with smirks on our faces) let our diatribe fly against her.

Chapter 7
I WANT MORE

Sundays after church are a time of fellowship with family and friends. Scores of people descend on us like a flock of crows in carloads from as far away as Philadelphia to enjoy Mother's famous cooking and delicious homemade breads and pies. Many see my father as a gracious, hospitable host who enjoys the fellowship of family members and friends, but I disagree. It annoys me that Father wants and needs the focused attention of all these other people, when it is Mother who carries the full weight of this almost weekly event. So much for Sunday being a day of rest. Father's only contributions to these events are to skillfully play Pinochle and to smoke good cigars once guests arrive. On the other hand, Mother and we children cook and can ceaselessly for the large crowd. She will be up late into the night on Saturday evening and well into Sunday morning in order to finish baking an extra ten to twenty scrumptious pies, in addition to the five she bakes almost daily for us. In the beginning, I enjoyed seeing cousins and church friends, but very quickly all the extra work and clean up that is required made me dread their arrival.

There are many other occasions besides just after church when family and friends come to our farm. On any weekend holiday, we have about forty-five people residing with us. People sleep everywhere, including inside the barns. There is always a lot of loud card playing and hearty drinking. My father loves, loves, loves to play Pinochle, and he loves, loves, loves to drink wine and beer. This makes his favorite pastime drinking alcohol while playing the game of Pinochle. I should be drinking too, but I don't mean the alcoholic kind. I mean that I should be drinking in the visiting laughter and happy chatter, but instead I am Schlechta Wanda. I can't help it. Memories of my weary mother wiping sweat and flour off of her furrowed forehead as she pushes yet another pie into the stove make me feel angry at the world and sorry for poor, exhausted Mother. I am sometimes bitter, mean, and irritable towards a few of the seemingly ungrateful and unsuspecting visitors who unluckily head my way. Mother says she prays that one day I will develop a true servant's heart. She explains that by *servant's heart*, she means that I will choose to do selfless things simply in order to help others and to make them happy without expecting anything at all in return. But for now, as a physically exhausted child on the Konschak farm, the very last thing that I want to do is to serve anybody else anything. I would much prefer showing them the door and then going to take a much needed but notoriously elusive nap.

The only times when I don't mind the extra work burden quite as much are when the company coming to our farm consists of the nearby farmers and their families. This is because they are arriving to assist us when it is our turn to have the thrashing machine. These people always reciprocate. We help them when it is their turn with the massive thrasher, and then, they assist us. After cutting, bundling, and shucking the golden wheat until it is dried out, it is time for us to get the thrasher. It is a gigantic machine that has two big parts to it and resembles a locomotive. It is owned by one rich businessman and rented out by the farmers. The thrasher blows the straw into a mammoth pile, and the wheat comes out of another section and goes into the waiting wagons or trucks and is taken to the empty barns. For a day and a half to two days, the giant machine is at our farm thrashing before moving on to the next expectant farmer. The farmers follow the machine and help each other. When it is our turn, there are so many people to eat the noon day meal in our spacious kitchen that we have to squeeze multiple other tables inside along with setting up additional tables on the porch. Even though we serve the food in two separate shifts, we still have to include all the extra seating. These things are a great deal of work, but at least it is only a day or two before another family has to feed everybody. At least for those days and nights that Mother basically lives in the kitchen, our family is being compensated with barns of overflowing grain and with the camaraderie created between neighbors and friends all working towards a similar goal of farming survival. Regardless of this positive experience, watching my mother being subjected daily to the never-ceasing demands of being a farmer's wife makes me ache for her and spurs me to want to lessen her crushing load.

That ache is probably where it all began. It is the birth of my dreams of getting off the farm and doing more with my life. Even though I love to have my hands in the dirt giving life to tiny seeds that would never grow without my attention, I don't need a huge farm to do that. I know that by using my brain and through hard work, I can have a career or a business of my own. Planting a garden could be something I do because I want to grow things, not because I have to produce crops to survive. I can have a job out in the world and still be a mother. I definitely don't want eleven children like my mother has birthed; three or four will be fine. Let's face it. One of the main reasons farming families are so large is because they need the children to work the farms and to take over once the patriarch and matriarch are too feeble. I have no intention of being the matriarch of a huge farm and working myself to death. I don't *need* to have a lot of children, and I sure as hell don't want a controlling husband. Mother is right. There is a lot of feistiness in me.

I recognize that education will be my method of escape. Schooling has always been easy for me. Typically, I'm not allowed to start school until almost November. Yet even with all of the days Father makes us miss school to work because "the farm comes first," I never fall behind in my lessons. My brothers and sisters and I used to go to Fairview School a mile south of our farm. It was a one-room schoolhouse where one overwhelmed teacher taught all eight grades. I must have been pretty cute because it seemed that all the male teacher wanted to do was to drag me up to his desk and have me sit on it during recess time. Emma, who was six years older than I, got fed up. She probably sensed that something wasn't quite right or at the very least felt badly for her little sister who never got to go outside to play. She came storming back into the school room one day during recess bravely yelling at our surprised teacher, "You big bum! You leave my baby sister alone!" For that outburst, she had to stay inside during recess for a whole week, but I finally got to go out. She made me proud to be her sister. Emma wasn't going to let anyone hurt me or hold me back if she could do something about it.

From first grade on, I have been asked to tutor children who are slower to catch on to new skills. I thoroughly enjoy helping them. After first attending Fairview for a couple of years, I went to a new, much larger, two-story school in Hartly. That only continued for a short time because some big jerk burned the school down. We children then had to walk to a church to have our classes until another school could be completed. Wealthy Mr. Pierre S. du Pont of the DuPont company graciously paid to have our new school built, and it is a glorious place that even has a fully stocked library and actual bathrooms.

When I know that we are going to be allowed to go to school, I excitedly shoot out of bed right after 4:00 a.m. and run to feed the chickens and milk my cows. We kids know what we have to do regarding the animals every morning, so we all obediently do our chores without question. We then charge back into the house for a fast, hearty breakfast. If it is still warm, like until October or in early spring, we also have to do field work before leaving for school. When we hear the train whistle blow at a quarter to eight, we quickly sprint back from the fields to the house, hurry to change our clothes, and scurry all the way to school three quarters of a mile away. This is all done by 9:00 a.m. Is it any wonder that I have grown up treasuring the loud refrain of a train whistle? That whistling sound means so much to me. It symbolizes freedom, challenge, and opportunity.

One day the principal of the school, Mr. Joodie, asked two other students and me to stay after school and help the teacher clean the boards and erasers and pack up and move some books. I told Richard to tell Mom that I would be home to do my after-school chores in an hour or two because I was staying to assist the teacher. I arrived home about an hour later than normal and was immediately grabbed by my father and roughly thrown down into the root cellar with the door viciously locked behind me. I cowered in the dirt part of the cellar where I'd landed in the area used to keep cabbage in the winter. The dark, dank cellar pressed against me and I struggled to keep my face from touching the dirt side. It was nearly impossible to calm myself as I felt the small, black space smothering me; its cold, thick fingers were encircling my throat. I couldn't breathe. Surely, I would soon suffocate. I began talking out loud quietly to myself. "The Lord is my shepherd; I shall not want. He maketh me to lie down in green pastures, he leadeth me beside still waters, he restoreth my soul." I willed myself to imagine lying atop green grass near a placid lake instead of seeing my reality of being trapped underground in a dark pit. "He leadeth me in the paths of righteousness for His name's sake. Yea, though I walk through the valley of the shadow of death, I will fear no evil: for thou art with me; thy rod and thy staff, they comfort me." I attempted to slow my panicked breathing. "Thou preparest a table before me in the presence of my enemies. Thou anointest my head with oil; my cup runneth over. Surely goodness and mercy shall follow me all the days of my life, and I will dwell in the house of the Lord forever." I repeated this Psalm over and over again in my head trying to keep myself from succumbing to icy terror. What I really wanted to do was to scream loudly and to tell that bastard to let me out because I couldn't breathe in here, but I knew from experience that resisting my father would only prolong my suffering. It was so dark, so very dark down there under the ground. I would have given anything to be able to see. I would have given anything for a light.

After what seemed like an eternity, Father finally let me out and hissed that I was never again to stay late at school but must come straight home and get my work done on the farm. I was just so thankful to be out of the pit that I actually respectfully concurred to his demand. I am sure Mother would have let me out sooner, but she was feeling particularly poor that day and could barely function.

Since that dreadful punishment, I have been terribly claustrophobic and unable to remain for long in what I perceive to be small, cramped, or dark places. I can't even bear to have my face submerged in water for more than a quick second. I've found that if I do have my face in water, I feel like the liquid is smothering me, so I don't enjoy bathing or swimming. I am never going to put my face all the way under water ever again because when I do, I am right back there in the pitch-black cellar—alone, afraid, and angry.

But even the cellar abuse from my father cannot squelch my love and desire for school and for learning. I treasure every moment spent at school and revel in the thought of absorbing every book that I bring home. I read profusely and am constantly finishing and returning books in order to check out others. Father has no idea that I am deceitfully hiding all traces of literary and intellectual masterpieces from his selfish eyes. The irony of me being so good at being distinctly bad is not lost on me, and I chuckle to myself whenever I think of it.

Chapter 8

MY FATHER, THE CRUSHER OF DREAMS

I am graduating at the very top of my eighth-grade class. It is a fine and exciting day. I have to admit that I am proud of myself for having the highest grades and beating out all the boys. Considering how much schooling I've had to miss because Father kept me home for planting, plowing, and harvesting, it is rather impressive that I passed at all, much less excelled. Mr. Joodie really wants me to continue my education. He says I have "great potential and a bright future." I can barely wait to further my schooling, and I look forward to walking to Hartly and taking the bus the rest of the way to the high school as my older siblings have done.

But I should have known that Father would never put my dreams before his wants. Why am I shocked when instead of congratulating me, Father says that I am now done with school? It is my worst nightmare, and I can't wake up from it. In defeated disbelief, I share this devastating information with Mr. Joodie. He looks truly horrified to hear that Father told me my schooling is finished.

It is a humid Sunday evening about a week later, and I am surprised to hear the dear voice of Mr. Joodie wafting up the stairs. He has come to speak to Father. I silently glide downstairs and hide in the gloomy shadows of the long hallway parallel to the sitting room. I can hear the whole strained conversation. My former principal really is convincing and makes several powerful points regarding why I should be allowed to continue my education.

"I can't. I can't," Father keeps repeating.

Mr. Joodie won't back down. "You have got to send this girl to high school! Wanda has got a great deal of potential," Mr. Joodie begs. I become hopeful that Father might relent. Mother also tries to help me.

"Don't you think it would be possible for Wanda to attend school some and to work the farm?" she interjects.

"No, it would not," answers Father.

Mother continues, "Well, maybe she could . . ."

"No!" Father interrupts. He then raises his voice towards Mr. Joodie saying, "Somebody has to help Mom, and she is the best one to help Mom."

Mr. Joodie makes one final weakened attempt. "You really should send Wanda to high school," he whispers.

My father's voice gets even louder. "Wanda is not returning to school! Mr. Joodie, I will not be changing my mind! Wanda will remain permanently at home to work the farm! Goodnight!"

I immediately feel a physical pain in my core like someone has stabbed me in the gut with a pitchfork. How can I even attempt to describe the absolute horror that I am feeling as I stand here hiding behind the wood and plaster wall of the hallway? I breathe in the agony of full understanding and nearly choke on it. The violent blow of how callously I am being pilfered from and how selfishly I am being used hits me full force. Father needs me to work the farm for him. He needs me to continue making him successful and rich; so, without a second's hesitation, mercy, or sorrow, my father steals from me my education, my future, and my dreams of all that I can be and do in this world. God made me intelligent, gave me a gift, and my father just crushed that gift under the heavy heels of his working boots, and I know he won't ever look back. For one quick moment, I peer around the cold wall and catch the sorrowful eyes of Mr. Joodie as he is led out of the room by my mother. In his eyes, I see reflected the grief I feel encircling my own pierced heart. All I can do tonight, as I muffle my heavy sobs with my feather pillow, is to pray to God to please help me. "Please help me Lord! Please help me!"

The next day I can't help but notice how nice Richard and Albert are being to me. I suppose that the story of my banishment to the farm has made the rounds through my siblings who understand what it is to have a dream and to watch it die. Later in the evening when I exit the house to dump out the dirty wash water soiled by the mounds of greasy dishes, my brother John Jr. follows me around the side of the house nearest to Mother's lovely rose bushes. He has a look of disturbance on his tanned face.

"Wanda," he stammers. "I'm real sorry that Father won't let you go to school. I knows you always been so smart and mighty quick to catch onto things. I used to be jealous of the way you known all the answers and could help Richard with his homework even though you was younger than him. Me dropping out of school is no big thing cause God's given me smart hands to fix things and make things run, and I gonna be just fine here. But you need more Wanda and it be a waste for you to be here. I be sad fer ya. I be sad." With those words, he hangs his head wearily. Dear, sweet Johnny. I know that he's opened his heart to me and out has tumbled such profound verbiage. This memorable day, my brother, who "was never quite right" and "is slow" and "simple minded," has spoken some of the wisest words I've ever heard. I hug him tightly and bury my face in the front of his dirty shirt.

"Don't worry about me Johnny. The Lord will provide." I say these words mainly to console him but am surprised when they console me also. As we turn to walk slowly back into the farmhouse, I feel a tiny flicker of hope ignite within me.

Chapter 9
MOTHER'S DEMISE

It has been a long, slow process, but it is becoming more and more obvious that Mother is putting on weight. Every part of her, from her toes to her face, has become bigger and bloated like a balloon stretched to its limit but unable to deflate. She is still beautiful, just rounder, plumper, and devoid of sharp edges. I also know that she bleeds constantly and never seems to have a reprieve from it. My guess, after skimming some medical books that I located in the school library, is that she has severe female issues along with some type of thyroid disorder, diabetes, or maybe even cancer. I distinctly remember one morning a while back when she hugged me before I went out to gather the eggs. I squeezed her arms as she pulled me towards her large, warm chest. They felt mushy like oatmeal, which struck me as a bit strange. I rested my head on her for a moment while she gently stroked the side of my face. "I love you Wanda," she whispered softly into my ear. I gave her one last *I love you too* squeeze before letting my arms go limp and stepping back to smile up at her. It was then that I noticed that there were still indentations on her arms where my fingers had pressed before we hugged. I was reminded of a soaking wet, cleaning sponge that stays squished together long after I've firmly squeezed it.

It is only recently that I've come to recognize how my handprints on Mother's arms are a troubling indication that something isn't quite right with her. They now seem eerily prophetic of my growing need and desire to keep my mother nearby. I wonder if she senses my increasing worry?

I feel like it is evident to everyone except Father and Grandmother that Mother's health is deteriorating. One late night, I hear my parents loudly arguing about whether or not the doctor should be called. Father clearly wins because no doctor arrives. Bam! With sudden clarity, I fully understand everything. Father's selfish manipulation in keeping me on the farm, instead of allowing me to attend high school like Paula, directly coincides with my mother's noticeably declining health. He understands that Mother's constant bleeding is foreshadowing her ultimate demise, and that good-for-nothing snake is ensuring that I will be ready to take her place. He must have somebody, other than himself, to help Mom. Without ever discussing it with me, he has decided that the best one to help her and to eventually replace her is obviously Schlechta Wanda.

My vicious grandmother uses my mother's physical downfall to her advantage, constantly teasing Mother about being "as fat as our biggest pink sow" and "obese like a pregnant cow." These are words that I know eat away at my mother and words that she doesn't feel she can refute. Father often joins in with this verbal abuse and laughs wickedly along with his mother as they concoct new similes.

One March evening about three weeks ago, after my father had joined Grandmother in berating my mother, he went outside to check on something in one of the barns. I decided that I could not stand to have Mother bullied any longer. If I had known that

Grandmother Theresa was soon going to die on April 1, 1923, I wouldn't have done anything, but of course, I didn't know the future and my need to protect Mother from the demoralizing present was too great. As soon as my mother darted out of the kitchen to go work on her endless pile of sewing, I stormed over to Grandmother's rocking chair, parked near the warm stove, and grabbed her arm. I yanked her up by her bony elbow and stuck my turbulent face right in front of hers.

"How dare you Schlechta . . ." she started to shriek, but I cut her off.

"If I ever hear you making fun of my mother again, I will hurt you," I said in a surprisingly calm voice that balanced on the edge of insanity. I pulled her even closer to my face, her rank coffee breath covering my nostrils, and repeated more slowly, "I—will—hurt—you."

She knew that I meant it and stopped the torturous insults of Mother, at least when I was around, but not before getting her revenge. She immediately told Father about what I had done, no doubt using some hyperbole, which was completely unnecessary in this case because the truth was bad enough. The next evening when I had my guard down, Father grabbed my right arm from behind and twisted it painfully as he dragged me out the back door of the kitchen. In a split second, he removed his leather belt; there was no escaping the wrath that rained down on my buttocks, legs, back, and shoulders. The brutal stings made me gasp in agony, but I did not give him the sick satisfaction of hearing me scream while he beat me. Again and again the belt buckle burned and cut into my flesh. *God help me, God help me*, my brain thought as I began to will myself to drift into unconsciousness. Mother was sometimes nearby and could save us from Father, but she wasn't around to save me this time. The agonizing hurt was so bad that I couldn't focus.

All I could discern were the colors black and red. It was with fascination, accompanied by shame, that I recognized what I was seeing as the blackness of the pain and the redness of my blood and hate.

As the months continue to pass, Mother's plump frame is unmistakable. Her rotund body seems an oxymoron to her pained, shrinking eyes. The dark circles under her bottom lashes are beginning to match her dark hair. Even though she continues to gain weight, I notice that she is eating less and less and that doesn't make any sense to me. Paula has been going to high school in Smyrna, but even she has to stop since Mother is becoming increasingly physically weak and in Father's words *useless*. Father sees that I can't do everything fast enough all by myself, so he forces Paula, who is the oldest daughter still living on the farm, to drop out of school too. It means that she now has to do the cooking while Mother supervises her. Paula also starts helping me with housework and cleaning and even sometimes picking in the fields.

When Paula turns eighteen, Mother selflessly advises her to go to Philadelphia where my sisters Jule and Emma are living. Mother tells Paula that there is nothing left for her on the farm and that "Wanda can do it all very well," and she is right. It isn't long before Paula starts working for a wealthy family in Elkin Park, Pennsylvania, doing cooking, cleaning, and chores. I am jealous. I want to go too but am deemed too young. I really wouldn't leave Mother anyway, but I want to be given the opportunity. Once Paula is gone, I only have two older brothers and no older sisters left on the farm, and I miss the others terribly. Their absence eats me up. I selfishly hope that Paula will come back home to be with me. It is a foolish wish.

Mother is barely able to leave her room since Paula left, so I immediately become the surrogate mother. I obediently do everything that my mother once did, minus her wifely responsibilities when sharing Father's bed. She seems relieved and yet regretful (for my sake) that I can take her place. It seems to me like my life is a recurring nightmare that I can't break free from and that there is no redo switch as my father sees that most of my older siblings—Gus, Jule, Bill, Emma, and now Paula—are long gone from the farm and making the most of their new lives in Philadelphia. I remain as the oldest of the two remaining Konschak daughters and Mother's logical replacement. How can it be that once again I am allowed no choice, no voice, and no input in the matter? It is just understood that I will be the caretaker while continuing all my dreary housework and strenuous farm chores. Some of my jobs I enjoy and do with pride, but most of the time, I feel trapped and more like an indentured servant than a daughter. I just want Mother to get better, and in the meantime, I want to make her sickly life as enjoyable as possible. It is not in my nature to admit to myself that my dear Mother is soon going to die.

Mother seems to sense her own death as she calls each of us children into her bedroom to speak to us alone. I don't know what words she shares with my siblings. I suspect that she has similar requests of us all. One afternoon, it is my turn. I hear Mother calling me. "Wanda. Wanda. Please come here so I can talk to you." I walk down the hallway like a criminal on death row afraid that it might be one of the last times I see her alive. Mother pats the motley quilt on her bed, indicating that she wants me to sit. Her head is sunken deeply into the soft, feather pillow. She begins, "Wanda, I know that it will be very hard for you once I am gone. Pray to God to lead you. He will provide!" She nods her head affirming her own words. "There is a great deal of the Konschak feisty nature in you, which can be both a blessing and a curse," she sighs. "You must use it as a blessing. You must use it to get through this life." I recognize words from the Bible as she continues to speak. "In the darkest night, remember that joy comes in the morning," she whispers while squeezing my hand lovingly. She ends with, "The Lord will provide! The Lord will provide!"

It is two weeks later that Father finally calls the doctor to our house. My parents' solid bedroom door closes quietly as the doctor goes inside to examine Mother. It takes a very long time, or at least it seems like it does, before he comes back out to furiously reprimand my father. I can't see anything from my perch on the stairs, but I can hear clearly. With obvious anger and disgust in his voice the doctor yells, "I might have been able to do something IF you had called me sooner!" I imagine the doctor's eyes full of scolding as they meet my father's. I will never forget those horrible words: *If you had called me sooner!* And there you have it. My father didn't want to spend his precious money to get a doctor for my mother. Health or money? He chose money. Father will, no doubt, come to be very sorry for his choice because I believe it will *cost* him a lot more than he is anticipating. The price will be his wife's life, and the interest paid may be losing the enjoyment of his own.

It is customary for the viewing of the body to take place in the home, so Mother's casket is placed in the living room in front of a large window framed by pale green curtains. I vaguely remember family and friends coming in and going out bringing us bowls, plates, pails, and baskets of food. I focus on Mother's pretty face in the simple casket. Her dark, curly hair is perfectly combed, and I've made sure to put her bun exactly the way she likes it—towards the top of her head versus the nape of her neck. I know that Mother's body is merely an empty shell. It is worthless in death. Her spirit is what matters, and her soul is enjoying her Lord in heaven. It brings me great peace to know that my mother now has no pain, no heartache, and no exhaustion to weigh her down. There is not a doubt in my mind that she knew, accepted, and loved Jesus Christ. Her life on Earth is over, but her joy and peace are only beginning. For me and others who remain left behind, though, there is still much heartache and grief to bear.

John Jr., being the saint that he is, stays home to watch over the farm so all the rest of us can go to Mother's funeral and burial. I want to celebrate her life, but all I can do is despair in her death. Going through the expected motions does little to ease my overwhelming grief. The emotional pain is so great that I actually feel it physically. My weighted arms and legs are heavy and it takes all of my energy just to raise my head and look people in the eye. My mother is gone! She truly and honestly loved me, and she is gone! I try not to be bitter and to remind myself of the powerful and encouraging words that she left me with, but my heart is broken. As I sob into my pillow that night, my heart intensely aches, and I feel it so heavy, so very heavy within my chest. Sorrow floods over me like water out of a spicket. I am only a child, but I wish that I had died too. Mother's death was a long time coming, but it is still such a violent blow that I can't fathom recovering from it no matter how much time might pass. I try but can't fight off the vivid hatred that I feel towards my father. It is irrational, but I can't help but feel like it is all his fault that my treasured mother is dead. I keep remembering how my distraught emotions were overrun with rage during her funeral and how anger's strangling fingers caused me to gasp for air as I watched her plain, pine casket being lowered into the unforgiving earth. Stinging words bounce off my brain. "If you had called me sooner." "If you had called me sooner." I feel completely justified in my hatred, and Schlechta Wanda overtakes me.

Chapter 10
TWO NEW MOTHERS

It is 1932 and my precious mother, Pauline, is dead at the age of fifty-one, but I remain. Wanda still exists. I am a fifteen-year-old, scared, little girl who never lets anyone see anything except a feisty, powerful woman. There is no mutual understanding between my father and me. It is just assumed that I will permanently and completely take over all of Mother's responsibilities. I cook. I bake. I clean. I sow. I make sure that the farm runs smoothly, order and buy supplies, sell eggs and chickens, dote on Mother's rose garden, care for Martha, and try to care for Albert. Even though I am not much older than they are, I really become a kind of mother to them. There is a tremendous need for a motherly figure, and I become that person.

One of my many responsibilities is doing all of the canning. I've put up 300 quarts of various produce all by myself this summer. Today, I've been putting up fresh peaches for several hours and am speeding to get supper on the table by noontime. I go flying up the stairs to curl into a tight ball on my bed as soon as I'm finished. It is the first day of my hated period and just like every month, I am terribly sick with pain. I can't wait to get just a few moments of slight relief from my cramps, so I have taken a shot of brandy and now have my knees up to my chest hoping and praying for any minimizing of my discomfort. About twenty minutes later, I go back downstairs to see Father laying sleepily on his black, leather couch. I don't realize that he is watching me so closely until he hollers, "Are you all right? Do you have your period?"

"No Pop! I do not have it!" I yell back even though I am actually moved that he has noticed my pain and shown concern, or so I think. Regardless of his bold and unusual questioning, I definitely am not going to tell my father about such a personal thing, and I sure as hell am not going to appear in any way that he might perceive as weak. Showing weakness just makes me an easier target for his verbal and physical tirades. Still, I can't help but let myself smile a little and am just starting to enjoy the shocking, new feeling of him caring about me when, like a bomb, he quickly blows it all to bits.

With complete seriousness and absolutely oblivious to his own stark ignorance, he actually says these words to me: "If you do have your period, I won't be able to eat the peaches later because they won't keep."

"Why wouldn't they keep?" I dare to ask in an incredulous tone.

"The peaches won't keep because you won't be able to screw them closed tightly enough!" shouts Father sulkily.

I want so badly to scream at him and to tell him that is one of the most ridiculous and absurd things that I have ever heard. Does he seriously think that I won't have the strength to close the jars tightly enough? I guess he figures that the loss of blood will make me physically weaker. He clearly doesn't really care that I am suffering. I understand that he won't be thankful for my dedication and sacrifice, even if he finds out that I have done all of today's canning work while feeling like complete and total crap. The only thing that he is really interested in is having fresh, delicious peaches to eat in the frigid months of the coming winter. "Well, I don't have IT, so the peaches will be fine!" I bellow and storm out of the room. It is a lie. I know that the peaches will be perfectly fine regardless; although once again, as a result of my self-absorbed father, I am nowhere close to being fine.

Days continue passing, and when I finally lay my weary head down to sleep each night, I should feel good about all that I've accomplished that day. The gnawing howl within me won't be quieted. It continually reminds me that I want so much more for my life. A raw, pressing feeling is always present, forever strengthening my longing to have my mother back alive and standing beside me. If I can't have that, then at the very least, I want a life I can live to my full potential.

I admit that I bring some of my hardship and discontent onto myself. I am just too fussy, too picky, and too high-strung. One example of this is that every morning, after I finish making breakfast and feeding my family, I clean the entire kitchen. This includes scrubbing the 18' x 18' kitchen floor on my hands and knees after I've swept it. I know this scrubbing endeavor is pointless because by noon everyone will be back in my recently cleaned kitchen with mud, dirt, and straw seemingly oozing from their pores. They'll devour the aromatic supper I've prepared and leave their grime behind. Their new mess necessitates me having to scrub the wooden floor again after lunch. No one points out the futility of my fussiness (not that I would listen), and no one offers to help me either. Every day leaves me thinking that there is no way that I can work any harder, but the next day I somehow do. I also don't think that there is any way that I can be more tired, but I always am. Saying that my childhood is completely over would be an understatement. Let me simply and naively sum it all up by saying that I think my life can't get any worse, so it probably will.

My father goes to many church conventions, especially since Mother died. As a member of the church who sits on the board, there is very little that goes on within our church that Father isn't highly involved in somehow. Just three months after Mother's death, I first notice that he is starting to receive letters from one specific, church lady. She lives in the part of Wilmington, Delaware, that will later become well known for being the place where the prominent African-American lawyer and civil rights advocate, Louis Lorenzo Redding, is born. She appears to be a good Christian woman, and I hear a rumor that she has a son like our John. I assume that Father met her at one of his church conventions and don't think much of it. I mention their communications to my brother Gus's wife, Matilda, and she tells me to keep one of the letters before giving it to my father. The following Sunday when Gus and Matilda stop by to visit, I pull a confiscated letter out from my hiding spot. Matilda eagerly grabs it from me, opens it using steam from the coffee pot on the stove, and proceeds to read it aloud. It is in German, but since she was born in Germany, that poses no problem for her. There is nothing too juicy inside. It is just a respectable love letter from a Christian lady making her interest in my father quite clear. I think we'll just put the letter back into the envelope and reseal it, but Matilda walks over to the stove, lifts up the lid, and drops the letter into the gleaming fire. "Matilda, don't do that!" I gasp. But it is too late. The letter burns up quickly before my stunned eyes.

Matilda and I never mention the stolen letter again, and I never reveal to my father the part I played in its destruction. I don't confess any of it because I am too scared. Immediately, I really regret not telling my father the truth. The omission haunts me constantly, and I'm afraid that it will for the rest of my life. Since my father never got the lady's letter, he never answered nor replied to it. I assume that led the lady to determine that my father didn't feel the same way about her that she did about him. She must now believe that Father doesn't really want to continue pursuing a relationship with her, and it could cause a gaping rift that might break them up for good.

Her letters stop coming to the farm, and that is the end of their courtship. I have unwittingly altered my father's fate; and in doing that, I've undoubtedly changed the whole direction of my own life. I quickly realize that it's the *what ifs* that kill you. "What if Father had gotten the letter and known of the lady's deep interest in him?" "What if he had married her?" "What if that Christian lady had become my mother?" All I can say is that regret is a greedy and demanding demon. That one choice (holding on to a letter) and that one moment (deciding never to tell Father) changed the course of my life forever and are a continual source of angst.

Quite unexpectedly one day about six months after the break up, Father tells us that he is returning to Germany for several months. We all wonder why he would go back but don't really care much because his absence means a welcome relief. Imagine our shock and sharp disbelief when we hear that Father will be coming back to America with a new wife! It isn't just any wife either but his dead wife's widowed and much younger sister, whose previous husband had died in an elevator accident! My mother left her parents' home before this sister was even born, and she is a complete stranger to us. In our eyes, and in the eyes of our neighbors and friends, marrying your wife's sister is an obscene and incestuous thing to do, but our father has gone and done it anyway.

The fateful year is 1934, and our new mother/aunt is here on our farm to stay, regardless of how we kids feel about it. I would have tried to foil Father's plans, but it is too late now. When my father walks into the room with my new stepmother, Alma, I truly feel like I am in a bizarre trance for several, long minutes. There I stand in the warm kitchen blanching green beans. I stare at her. I wonder if my mouth gapes open; for once in my life, I am utterly speechless. We soon learn that Alma has a married daughter, Alvina, who has a one-year-old baby. I am flabbergasted when I find out that my father actually paid $1,500 to have Alma's daughter, son-in-law, and grandchild brought over to the United States. Father couldn't pay for a doctor for my suffering mother, but he can pay to bring three complete strangers across the ocean! I cannot fathom any rational explanations to warrant his decisions.

That first night with HER under our roof, insomnia sets in, and my thoughts race like those of a crazy person. I can't stop talking to myself. *What in the hell is Father thinking? Lazy, good for nothing; I am running the house! Why does he need Alma? Does he really want and need sex that badly that he's gotten married again just to supposedly have it? Why couldn't he just find a widow nearby? Why did he have to shame us all by going all the way back to Germany and marrying my mother's sister? Embarrassing rumors, accusations, and gossip will fly unimpeded all over Hartley now!*

I wonder if Alma started the whole affair by writing to my father and winning him over with her praises and sympathies? Had she, my aunt turned stepmother, played on Father's insecurities and loneliness, enticing him with promises she never intended to keep? My stream of consciousness thoughts are brutal and won't stop, but they are only the foretaste of the horror yet to come.

Alma and my mother could not be more opposite. Since my mother was gone from the household before Alma's birth, I know that Alma and my mother weren't ever close, and from what I understand, their upbringings were completely dissimilar. The older siblings, including my mother, were raised in a very religious and Godly home with church as an essential component. Alma, on the other hand, was not brought up within the church, scoffs at religion, and has no apparent faith in Jesus Christ. She is so much younger than my mother that she could be her daughter instead of her sister, and Alma's actions, attitude, and mannerisms are so unlike Mother's that she seems to have been raised by completely different parents. I pray to God to help me control my indignant emotions as Schlechta Wanda boils quickly to the surface every time Alma comes near me.

My questions about my stepmother and Father are not being answered, and my thoughts are not being appeased. I still don't know the whole story. In her defense, I hear that my father extravagantly wined and dined the much younger Alma while he was in Germany courting her. I know that he even bought her a very beautiful and very expensive fur coat that she loves to flaunt in my face. It seems highly plausible, therefore, that she expected her life as a new wife in America to be sharply different from what it actually ended up being. Perhaps her fantasies of being a rich, farmer's wife were a blindfold to the reality of actual farm life.

Nevertheless, I do know a few basic facts, and they are as follows: 1) My mother needlessly died in 1932 at the age of 51, 2) In 1934, my father returned to Germany to court and marry his widowed sister-in-law, Alma, and 3) Father thrust Alma on the rest of us without explanation and without pity. I am also of the knowledgeable opinion that my father already rues the moment he first intended to make Alma his new wife. He surely regrets bringing her nasty, nagging, cruel self to America after blindly and foolishly yoking himself to her before God for the rest of his life on Earth. His unilateral decision to deposit her into our lives pours salt into the open, raw wound that is my mother's absence and turns virtually every day into a living hell for us all.

Chapter 11
CINDERELLA AND THE MURDERING OF THE MUSIC

I know that many people are familiar with the popular fairy tale *Cinderella,* but most don't realize that a highly beloved early version of the story was a French folk tale written by Charles Perrault in 1697 called *Cendrillon*. Perrault's version contains an evil second wife who has two evil daughters. To my horror, I realize that I am the personification of Cinderella minus one stepsister. My real life terrifyingly mirrors the narrative. I truly do have an evil, vicious stepmother who makes me do all of the work while she and her lazy daughter sit around idly. I may unwittingly bring some of my suffering onto myself by being hesitant to hand over the reins of the household to this complete stranger. I still want to do things the way that I have always done them because I don't trust Alma to do them correctly. She is only too happy to oblige. Alma often expresses her beliefs to my father by stating, "You can't have two women in the house!" She is evidently choosing to allow me to be the woman of the house until she can find sufficient ways to get rid of me. Her hatred for me is palpable, and Albert says that her jealousy of my youth, looks, and considerable skills is blatant. Unfortunately for Schlechta Wanda, there is no sanctuary of a fairy godmother nor a stunning prince to come to my rescue. My real-life drama definitely does not end with "they lived happily ever after."

I feel like Alma despises all of us children, but she especially hates me. The first thing she ever said to me was, "Wanda, I need water heated and carried to my tub so I can take a bath!" No "please" or "nice to meet you." No "sorry you lost your mother." There is no warmth in her. I can use words like icy, ill-tempered, malevolent, vicious, truculent, and so on. But just let me sum it all up with one word—mean. My stepmother is mean. Maybe she can justify it to herself by saying she doesn't feel wanted or that America is not what she thought it would be. The fact still remains that she is downright, inescapably mean. Since the first moment she walked in, everything is all about her and what she needs. The only other person she cares about is her own biological daughter, Alvina, who of course never has to help out on the farm or do any tedious chores. It isn't just the fact that my evil stepmother never does anything to help me in the running of our farm, it is that she is hateful and curt every time she addresses me. Her commands are always spit out without any politeness or thanks. She quickly latches on to the *Schlechta Wanda* slogan as my feisty nature exerts itself. I do everything that she demands, but not always before finishing whatever job I am currently working on first. I complete her tasks thoroughly and with perfection, but I sometimes work slower than usual when I am around her. I even follow her ridiculous requests regarding things like how to fluff her pillow *just so* and how to leave only one side of the top sheet rolled down when I change their bed. And yet, I am unable to do these things without occasionally making cleverly snide comments or rolling my eyes. This causes her to glare at me in an even more frightening manner (if that is even possible) and eventually leads to unavoidable, albeit nasty, bickering between us. She often makes fun of me and the rest of my family for our Christian faith. "My daughter and I laugh at all the church going you do," she snickers. I prepare myself for the oncoming philippic that always follows and try to remain calm. Alma is what we nowadays call "a regular Hitler all over." She is anti many things. Anti-Jew, anti-Gypsy, anti-Christian, and certainly anti-Wanda. My perception is that she's never gone to church, prayed, or espoused any religious beliefs whatsoever; at least I have never seen her do any of these things since she came. Whether I am asleep or whether I am awake, I can never escape the deep crease between Alma's black eyebrows nor the vacant, angry look in her dead eyes. Alma's eyes are so very unlike my mother's eyes that danced and sparkled with life.

Poor Martha doesn't fare much better. Like me, Martha had a close bond with our mother. When Martha was only four years old, Father insisted that she should start her farm work. "After all," he stated, "she is another mouth to feed!" Mother would not hear of it. She insisted that Martha wait until she was six before she started doing work on the farm. The day after Martha turned six, she started her job at 4:30 a.m. and waved goodbye to free time and fun. From then on, Father ordained that she help feed the 3,000 baby chicks before leaving for school by sled in the winter or by horse and wagon in good weather. She had to assiduously clean the stinky chicken coops and to feed the chickens again after school before rushing into the house to practice her music. Martha was twelve when Mother died, and as soon as our mother was gone, Father immediately ended Martha's piano lessons saying, "Twenty-five cents a lesson is too expensive!" He had never wanted to spend his precious money on her lessons, but he had done so since Martha was five years old because of Mother. I don't know what kind of deal Mother had to make with him or what she had to do in exchange. It was clear that Mother wanted her last child, her baby, to have piano lessons, especially after it became apparent that Martha was a natural who thoroughly enjoyed not only playing but also practicing for hours and hours. I am sorry to say that it sometimes annoyed me that Martha could get out of chores by begging Mother to let her practice on the organ. Year-round, Martha serenaded us as we worked in the chicken houses, barns, gardens, and fields. I particularly loved Martha's music in the summer when all the farmhouse windows were open wide to allow the fragrance infused air to enter. Her beautiful piano music was then readily heard as it easily escaped into the outside world. But all of that ended upon Alma's arrival.

Now that Alma is with us, she often yells at Martha to "stop playing that organ" whenever Martha finds a few fleeting moments to practice a song. Martha quickly learns that trying to play the organ results in her being given additional, despicable chores and work tasks to complete. Even more than this obvious punishment, I think Martha wants to avoid the bitter, incessant raised voice of our stepmother. So along with losing our mother, who always comforted her and made things better after Father whipped her good, Martha also has to endure the pain of giving up her beloved piano playing. Martha's tremendous talent is abandoned and wasted as all music in our house dies because my father and Alma kill it.

Albert is blessed when it comes to Alma because, for the most part, she ignores him. She isn't downright mean to him like she is to Martha and me. He is able to stay clear of her a majority of the time, and he does his best to do so. He says that she was overly friendly to him at first but then quickly changed to being nasty. He also says that it is way too easy for her to quickly become malevolent. That is why he avoids her like the plague. Avoidance is much more difficult for us girls because a lot of our chores are done in the house where Alma loiters pointlessly most days. Like the rest of us, Albert also finds our stepsister, Alvina, to be truly terrible. He does his best to avoid her too. Alvina's personality is very much like her mother's, and in my opinion that is definitely not a good thing. She really never has anything to do with us nor we with her. Alvina is a stranger even though she is our cousin turned stepsister. Perhaps we should try harder to befriend her, but I promise that she makes it nearly impossible. When people in town talk about her being trashy, I don't feel the need or desire to defend her, which in itself should tell you a lot.

Chapter 12
BABY BROTHER ALBERT

Baby brother Albert. He hates when I call him "baby" brother since he is only two years younger than me. But he is indeed younger, as I like pointing out, and therefore a baby compared to me. Albert is and always was ornery, so very ornery! I had to walk him to school when he was little, and there was many a morning when he would just lie down in a random field that suited him and commence to kicking his legs furiously. I would go to yank him up, and his stubby arms would flail. He absolutely refused to go. I'd yell and cuss and struggle to get him on his feet all the while screaming, "I don't have time for this crap!" After much effort, we'd be on our way. I secretly enjoy when Albert is ornery to the rest of the family because it shows that he too is schlecht. In that way, he is really quite wonderful. We may fight a lot and often greatly irk each other, but we are very close and understand one other in a deep and powerful way, especially when it comes to our dealings with Father.

Like all the rest of us, Albert had to start working on the farm at a very young age. He has always been an extremely hard worker and possesses a way of *talking* to the animals that many times makes them more agreeable. I think that Albert is often more at ease around animals than he is people. For animals, he is even willing to risk getting a beating from our father; for example, he looks the other way when Martha hides the kittens. Martha loves all the animals, and when the cats have too many kittens for my father's liking, she will quickly gather them up and hide them before Father can drown them or make Albert drown them. Albert never says a word about Martha's traitorous deeds and looks relieved to witness the growth of the multi-colored fluff balls into cantankerous adult cats.

Albert has always really loved tending to the animals. Mother had hardily encouraged him to become a veterinarian, and I concurred deeming it a splendid idea. Being a veterinarian would get Albert off of the farm and away from our father while still letting him be surrounded by a part of farming that he really loved. I am sure that Albert would indeed have become a veterinarian if our mother hadn't died. It is beyond unfortunate that in the winter of his eleventh-grade year, my father and Alma forced him to quit school in order to work full-time on the farm. They fully accomplished this by diabolically hiding all of Albert's shoes, thereby making it impossible for him to attend school because of the freezing temperatures and thick snow. With their treachery, Alma and Father snuffed out Albert's lofty flame and sat around cackling about it like witches surrounding a black cauldron of evil brew. Their stealing of Albert's shoes is what ended his scholastic education and his well-deserved dreams of becoming a vet. The utter cruelty of it all makes me visibly shudder.

On a happier note, Albert loves to tell his friends the story about when he was rescued by his horse. Albert has a particular work horse named Thunder that he dotes on daily. Any spare moments that he has will be spent with that massive horse. Albert spoils Thunder by feeding him fresh garden carrots and bright red orchard apples, by frequently brushing his light brown mane, and by secretly riding him after feeding him his daily oats. While Mother was still alive, Richard, Albert, and Martha sometimes used to sneak away from their chores and ride the work horses together. Albert says that once in a while when he and Thunder are together, they startle deer that have come to enjoy the tasty plants and crops. It amuses him when Thunder, the gentle giant, timidly tries to follow the frightened deer back into the thick clumps of emerald trees from which they've emerged.

The day that Albert almost died was a pleasantly warm and breezy day. Albert was in the cow pound checking on two heifers that had recently given birth to adorable black and white calves with huge, brown eyes and curly, black lashes. Unbeknownst to Albert, a mammoth-sized bull had broken his restraints in the main barn and had followed the fence up to the upper portion of the cow pound. Something told Albert to look up, and that's when he saw the tremendous bull. The huge, angry creature was full of ardor for Albert, the interloper, so it came charging down the hill straight for him. In the split second it took to consider his options, Albert knew that it was too late for him to sprint to the fence and climb over it. A bull goring was a hideous, bloody thing that most people didn't survive, and Albert knew he was doomed. He was too far from the fence, and there was nothing between him and the gigantic bull. There was nowhere to hide, nothing to climb up onto or to dart behind, and not enough time left to run far enough away, or so he thought. The next thing Albert registered was the form of Thunder coming between him and the charging bull. Albert's shy horse had run up between Albert and the bull and was neighing furiously while rising up on its muscular back legs. Thunder, acting as a blockade, was more than a distraction to the possessed bull. He was the life saver that Albert needed to give him time to get out of the muddy cow pound alive. My short and stocky brother ran like an Olympic champion and catapulted himself over the fence rail towards survival. Thunder had been willing to die for Albert. What an amazing horse and what a special friendship, not to mention a fantastically thrilling story.

Thank God Thunder didn't have to give his life in exchange for my brother's because that horse's death would have completely destroyed Albert. After enduring our mother's death, he could never have withstood the untimely death of his beloved horse. Mother had favored Albert as her youngest baby boy and had saved him from many a beating from our father. When she died, there was no one to completely replace her motherly affection towards him, even though I tried to be the best caretaker and surrogate mother that I could. I know that he appreciates my good intentions and efforts, but of course, it can never really be the same. His heart, like mine, is broken. Albert's bitterness would have overcome and obliterated him like smoke from a raging fire if Thunder had been killed. I have no doubt that God knew that and spared both Albert and Thunder that afternoon. It is truly a miracle and a blessing that the two of them are unhurt and can go on to have several more years of farm work and fun escapades together.

Chapter 13
NEVER MESS WITH MARTHA'S HAIR

I am strong and rightfully tough, but my brother Albert is stronger. His physical strength is noteworthy and impressive, even to me, and I am not easily impressed. The only advantage I have is that I am older, which equates to being more experienced. When we wrestle or outright fight physically, I sometimes am able to win. Interestingly enough, I am the one who taught Albert how to be a better fighter. He, in turn, taught Martha how to be a genuinely excellent fighter. Martha is younger and smaller than me; I guess it would be correct to call her small-boned. Her sprite-like appearance leads to many a naive boy misjudging her superior fighting capabilities. They learn through black eyes and bruises that Martha is a great deal stronger than she looks. Boys at school who are bullied by other boys even seek her out to fight for them, which she always does and always wins. Martha's only complaint after victory is that fighting messes up her hair that I expertly fix for her every morning. Suffice it to say that the three of us are a lethal fighting machine when it comes to battling for something we believe in or to defending the Konschak name. One of the best examples of our fighting skills being put to the test happened on a chilly, fall afternoon as we walked home from church youth group.

I was having a debate with Albert regarding Columbus "discovering" America when it was actually already occupied by the Native American Indians. It seemed ridiculous to me that our schoolbooks didn't acknowledge the absurdity of promoting Columbus while ignoring the long established existence of Indians. Martha shuffled along a few feet behind us interjecting her thoughts into our heated discussion. Four boys, who lived on a smaller farm near ours, walked along beside us. Finding a lull in our conversation, Thomas, the oldest and tallest brother, stepped directly in front of Albert who then inadvertently bumped into him.

"Oh, so little, rich boy can't see where he's going? You ran into me!" Thomas barked.

"Well, I wouldn't have run into you if you hadn't stepped right in front of me," answered Albert.

"I can tell that you think you're better than me just because your farm is bigger!" Thomas spit out.

"What are you even talking about? I never said that, and I don't think that," said Albert.

Thomas wouldn't back down. He leaned forward and rammed one of his pointer fingers into Albert's chest before responding. "But you do think that it's okay for your incestuous father to marry the sister of his fat, dead wife?"

Albert's face turned red as he took two steps back to distance himself from Thomas. I saw him ball up his fists and knew he was ready to fight. Now, as I said, I could sometimes beat up Albert, but I sure as hell was not going to let anyone else do it. Even more than that, I was not going to allow that "fat" comment about my deceased mother to go unpunished. Plus, in all actuality, the Konschak farm was a great deal larger and more successful than Thomas's father's farm, but we had never, ever lorded that over him. At that same moment, the other three brothers sealed their fates when one of them ruffled and then yanked Martha's hair before shoving her to the ground, while the other two pushed Albert from behind sending him hurling towards Thomas. Thomas used that opportune moment to punch my innocent brother in the face. What an inspirational example it would be if I could say that I held fast to the prophetic message given at youth group only an hour before: "Blessed are the peacemakers, for they will be called children of God." But the only kind of peace that I was going to be making would come much later that night when I asked God for forgiveness.

Immediately after I witnessed Thomas's physical attack on Albert, I let Schlechta Wanda fly free, and it felt good. I sprang towards Thomas and punched him as forcibly as I could in the gut. As he bent forward clutching his stomach, I gave him no time to recover before punching him directly in his unsuspecting face. I hadn't intentionally aimed for his nose, but that's what I got. He staggered back in shock and fell to his knees covering his face with his hands while dark, red blood streamed out of his nostrils. I figured that he was done and turned my attention to Martha, but she didn't need my help. When I first saw her, she was sitting on top of one of the younger brothers who was on the ground. Martha was pulling his hair like he had first done to her seconds before. In an ill-conceived attempt to get her to stop, he began screaming obscenities interjected with references to our mother. Martha immediately jumped up to her feet and kicked him hard between the legs. "That's for my mother!" she screamed. He curled into a tight ball and began rolling side to side in silence. Meanwhile, Albert was fighting the two remaining brothers who had unfairly ganged up on him.

Punches were flying wildly, and I jumped into the middle of it only to be punched in the mouth. I tasted salty blood on my lips but kept swinging. Albert caught sight of my bloody face and hurled himself at my attacker, tackling him like an opponent in a football game. The boy hit the ground with a thud, gasped for breath, and laid still. That left one brother standing, and Albert, Martha, and I glared at him simultaneously causing him to turn around and run rapidly towards his farm without once looking back.

The three of us then proceeded victoriously on our way to our own farm leaving the defeated enemies who remained to recover on the dusty battlefield. No words were spoken; they didn't need to be. As we plodded up the road to our farmhouse, the first person to see us was Father. What he beheld was me with a busted, bloody lip, Albert with a blackening eye, and Martha dirty, with a torn shirt and completely messed up hair. I was pleasantly surprised when Father actually asked us what had happened. "Someone messed with Martha's hair," I said. Albert, Martha, and I then continued walking towards the barns and chicken runs to do our chores as if nothing had happened. It was a magnificent moment; one glorious episode that would live on in infamy for many years to come.

Chapter 14
HE MADE HIS BED

It is a pitch-black evening, and I can't sleep because of all the loud noise filtering up from the basement. I hear raised male voices, drunken laughter, and indiscriminate cursing. As I try unsuccessfully to block the disturbance by pulling my colorful quilt up over my face, I can't keep myself calm. I think about how ridiculous this is. Here I am trying to rest after a full and exhausting day, and my father and his friends are downstairs getting drunker and louder by the second. Some of us have to get up again in a few hours and don't have the luxury of playing card games and drinking all night!

I throw off the thick covers and jump up from my lumpy bed. The wood floor feels cool to my toasty warm feet as I stomp angrily down the stairs to the first story and turn resolutely to head towards the basement. I fling open the basement door and immediately begin yelling. "There has been more than enough drinking and carrying on for one night, so get the hell out of our house! Get out! Get out you bastards!" I repeat several German profanities for extra affect as I storm through the basement pulling grown men up out of their chairs by their shirt collars. There is no fear in me, and they recognize that. I am like Jesus when he chased the greedy money changers out of the Temple, except that I clearly am not blameless. I push and shove men towards the stairs and their brisk exit. I am barely more than a child, but I glare and curse like an adult and show no pity even when one drunkard falls while trying to escape me. I hear a few mumbles of "Schlecht Wanda," but soon the basement is completely empty except for my father and me. He just stands there and stares at me in a drunken stupor.

"Get upstairs and get to bed!" I shout while pointing towards the stair rail. It is then that I notice thick tears streaming out of Father's bloodshot eyes. He is crying! Not just crying but wailing like a baby!

"Alma, Alma," he sobs. "She is horrible! Life with her is terrible! Horrible. Horrible. But she was so pretty and young. She says that I am not enough man for her! Why did I bring her here? Oh, God! What did I do?" moans my father.

As I look at my fifty-seven-year-old father sobbing, for the first time in my life I see him as a fellow sufferer who is weak, vulnerable, deceived. He has made horrible mistakes, but haven't we all? Perhaps his own father was abusively strict and unloving towards him, so he just perpetuates what he knows. His drinking habits have greatly increased since Alma came to our home, and that makes perfect sense. He wants to block her out and to numb the pain she inflicts. For a brief moment, I truly feel sorry for Father, and empathy floods through me like water released from a dam. Then the old, malevolently poetic, created words "Schlechta Wanda, Schlechta, Schlechta, Schlechta Wanda," spew icily from his lips. Even in the midst of his drunken distress, my father is still ready to label me with the same brutal denouncement of my moral fiber that I have heard all of my life and to forcibly shove the thorny crown of badness onto my head.

"Go to bed Father," I whisper. The mercy that I felt for him is gone, erased, forgotten. Instead of forgiving him like I should, I bitterly focus on my former feelings, which are that he has brought it all on himself. Father walks dejectedly upstairs towards his bedroom where Alma waits for him in the darkness like a serpent in a hole, and I do not feel any pity. It is his own fault. He has made his bed, and now he can literally lie on it.

Chapter 15
THE JOY OF TWO SETS OF STAIRS

I am not the only child in my family who has learned how to use the two sets of stairs in our farmhouse to my advantage. The main stairs are wide and empty out into the parlor directly to the right of the front door. Guests always enter from this door and enjoy the fancier, albeit less comfortable, furniture arranged there. If you continue on further into the house, you enter the large kitchen. A second, narrower set of stairs is located there. This means that a fleeing child can run up the kitchen stairs, sprint down the upstairs hall, and plummet back down the main stairs into the decorated parlor. I eventually discovered that running up one set of stairs and down the other multiple times creates a virtual circle of exhaustion for my father when he is chasing me. I can't outrun him on level ground, but by adding the extra strain of climbing stairs, I am able to increase the distance between us with every ascension. When I have gained enough space to give me a few extra moments to fling open the front door and make a run for it, that's exactly what I do.

The first time I tried this tactic was on a typical, sticky morning at the beginning of summer. I was busy gathering, washing, weighing, and packing eggs. For some unknown reason, Father walked into one of our farm storage buildings where I happened to be stacking the egg crates. As I strained to carry another crate brimming over with eggs towards the door, I tripped. The floor was made of bricks and, therefore, somewhat uneven in places. Some of the bricks were higher up than others because the ground beneath them had shifted and settled. I couldn't see in front of me while carrying the crate, and the left toe of my boot rammed into the side of a brick that wasn't level with its mate. The rest of my body and the heavy crate of eggs kept going forward even though my left foot jerked to an immediate stop. As I fell, there was no way for me to protect the fragile eggs. Bam! The crate of precious eggs crashed onto the brick floor. Immediately, yellowish yokes oozed out from between the crate slits and spread out over the red floor like hungry tentacles. I felt a sharp pain in my right elbow, which had hit the ground first before both of my knees slammed down. As I attempted to sit up, I immediately felt blood dripping down my forearm. "Schlechta Wanda! What have you done?" my father roared. "This is going to cost me a fortune!"

If my father had not been there to witness my unfortunate mishap, I would just have cleaned everything up and gone about my business. The fact that he was present made that scenario impossible. I knew that I had to get away from the messy scene of the *crime* or endure a severe beating. Even though my kneecaps felt like they were shattered, I shot up and bolted out of the room. I ran towards the house, flinging open the back door and charging full force towards the kitchen stairs. Up, up, up I went and across the upstairs hall with Father right behind me. At the other end of the hallway, I sailed down the formal stairs and grabbed the final banister spindle with my left hand so that I could fling myself around it. Through the parlor I sprinted only to once again run up the kitchen stairs.

Around and around and around I went. Up and down, up and down, up and down three times before tiring Father enough to put myself a few feet in front of him. The whole while, he was furiously cursing me in German and demanding that I stop running, which I was definitely not going to do. Only an idiot would stop running. One of his large hands was outstretched to grab me, and the other monstrous hand clutched his leather belt that he had somehow already removed from his pants. He was so close behind at first that it seemed like his hot breath singed the hair on the back of my head. But thank the good Lord, every time I ascended the stairs, Father fell a little bit farther behind me. On my final descent, instead of propelling myself around the spindle, I aimed for the front door, which was open except for the screen. I flung the screen door wide and blasted outside towards the cornfields. I didn't look back. I knew that because I had been able to make it out the door without being grabbed, I had won. Father was thoroughly exhausted and now much too far behind me to have any hope of securing me before I hid amongst the infinite rows of sheltering corn. After reaching the middle of the corn field farthest from the house, I allowed myself to crumble onto the welcoming ground and rest. I was physically drained and bloody, breathing heavily as I licked my bone-dry lips dreaming of cold water. More importantly, though, I was victorious! I had escaped a whipping from Father as well as successfully outwitting him. I relaxed my muscles and smiled up at the glaring sun.

It was late that same evening when Albert and Martha snuck outside with some food that they had stolen from the kitchen. Since I had fallen asleep, I don't know how long they searched for me before I heard them yelling my name rather loudly. I was extremely grateful for the confiscated food and the tin pail of milk. I quickly crammed every morsel into my mouth. We all laid back with our arms underneath our heads and looked longingly up towards the twinkling, diamond stars. I thought about our Mom looking down on us with blessings and love, and I felt better. Maybe there were even angels and God himself smiling on us, their presence undetectable by our human eyes. Martha assured me that it would be safe to come home now because some of Father's friends had arrived unannounced at dinner and had stayed to drink heavily and play Pinochle. I pictured Father passed out on the kitchen couch, drool dangling from his bottom lip and one arm flung across his eyes to keep out any hint of light and a possible sighting of Alma. Knowing I'd be safe, I opted to return home with Albert and Martha. I could now get in a couple hours of placid rest on the down mattress that Mother had stuffed for me herself. It had been a pretty good day overall, but I was ready for it to be over. The three of us headed towards the dark, sleeping house. Images of how best to employ my brilliant, new stair tactic danced in my head. I knew that I would undoubtedly need them in the very near future. "Sigh."

Chapter 16

LORD JESUS FORGIVE ME

This is the third time this evening that I have tried to say my prayers but been overcome with laughter instead. I should really be ashamed, but I'm not. Earlier today, I was feeling particularly angry at Father because of a vicious beating he gave Albert yesterday. Father started the whole thing when he dictated that Albert finish plowing over an emptied cornfield even though it had just stopped pouring rain the size of ripe grapes, and there was standing water everywhere. Albert conceded but was unable to keep the horses and the plow from becoming hopelessly encased in mud. He was finally able to free the horses from the sucking, drenched earth, but the plow was completely stuck. Even Albert was knee deep in a brown river when I came to help him.

Snap! We heard it before we saw it. A piece of metal had broken off of one of the plow tips. That particular sharp piece had become wedged under a large rock hidden beneath the heavy mud, and when we pulled the plow upwards, it had snapped off. When Father found out about his damaged equipment, he was irate. He said that it was our fault for not doing a better job of stone picking. Stone picking is what we call going out into the fields year after year to pick up and remove the stones exposed by erosion that get in the way of planting crops. It is a tedious, boring job that never ends because there are always more rocks coming to the surface like blemishes on fine skin. Anyway, Father then changed his mind and decided that it was all Albert's fault because he had been the person plowing. It didn't matter that my father had been the one who unwisely forced Albert to plow in the rain drenched conditions in the first place; he decided that it was Albert who deserved to be thoroughly punished and wasted no time in making him pay.

It was so wrong and unfair, and I wanted to make it better for my stridently beaten brother. As I walked into the horse barn today to clean out Thunder's stall for Albert, I heard the sound of loud, obnoxious snoring. I turned to see my father in a drunken slumber with his back propped up against one of the wooden stall doors. One empty bottle of wine was in his lap and another next to his right hand. And then it hit me. What if that stall door was to suddenly open because it wasn't latched correctly? What if Father were to fall backwards into the dirty stall because there was no longer anything to hold him in an upright position while he slept? What if there just happened to be a gigantic pile of smelly, putrid horse manure right there where he fell? I knew that in the Bible God tells us, "Vengeance is mine." On this particular day, however, vengeance belonged to Schlechta Wanda. I grabbed a shovel and climbed silently over the railing and into the empty horse stall. I moved a load of the nastiest black poop into position making sure that it wasn't high enough to hinder the stall door from swinging fully open. The height from the barn floor to the stall's door gave me several inches of beautiful, stinky horse waste to work with. I climbed back over the top rail, replaced the shovel in its spot, and surveyed the latch above Father's resting head. Leaning in the direction I would be running, I reached my hand out and counted to myself—*One, two, three!*—before lifting the latch and sprinting out of the open barn door like a world champion runner. I knew it wouldn't take Father more than a few seconds to fall backwards into the glorious horse shit, but I figured it would take him a few minutes to actually wake up and orient himself to where he was and to what had happened. I hoped and prayed that once he was lying on his back in the horse stall, he wouldn't see me speedily fleeing the scene.

It was even better than I could have ever dreamed. I ran undetected into the house and up to Albert's room, where I encouraged my brother to look out his window and witness what I'd done. What he beheld was our father emerging from the barn covered in foul horse manure from the top of his head, down his spine, to below his waist. Thick clumps of dung slid off his back and were cascading down the backs of his legs like muddy waterfalls, creating a trail of fecal matter behind him. He was cussing ferociously and suddenly started spitting profusely in order to remove a watery piece of horse poop that had dripped down his forehead into his mouth. I almost gagged. Albert and I covered our mouths to keep from laughing too loudly and sat down beneath the window sill. The premier part of the whole thing was that it appeared to Father to be a complete accident. To him, this unlucky mishap was an act of nature or, more rightly, an act of God. He had gotten too drunk and fallen asleep while leaning on the door of a horse stall that wasn't completely latched. His weight had eventually opened the door, and he had fallen back into the ripe manure, or so he thought. He couldn't blame anyone but himself or God, and he surely wasn't going to blame God. I smiled at Albert and quietly started singing, "More rain, more rest. Father got shit on in the horse's nest. More rain, more rest. Father got shit on in the horse's nest." Lord Jesus forgive me! I just couldn't help myself. Maybe I really am Bad Wanda after all, and maybe that is not such a schlecht thing. John Konschak has created a monster that he can no longer contain, and I feel guilty, only because I don't feel guilty.

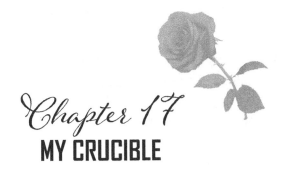

Chapter 17
MY CRUCIBLE

The story of how I was kicked off the farm riles me up whenever I have the unfortunate chance to relive it in my mind. Here it is for you to ponder and to learn from my mistakes. Please remember that anger is evil, and anger is exhausting. Even though I knew both of these things, I could not stop myself from being angry with Father and my stepmother. I felt daily like I was in Dante's deepest layer of hell as I found myself cornered by two people who I hated. In my defense, they hated me first; although, in the case of my father, it is probably more accurate to say that he just didn't care enough about me to be bothered. He couldn't outright hate anything or anyone as profitable to himself as me. I was too valuable of an asset to be loathed. My stepmother, on the other hand, despised me and was a germinating danger. Her cruel verbal and emotional abuse—Cinderella and I had way too much in common—continued to get worse. Despite that, I was pleased to realize that I no longer feared for my physical safety around Father because he was now usually much too drunk to pose any kind of a menacing threat. My stepmother, though, was a patient conspirator plotting my downfall. She was a greater hazard than I could ever have imagined.

One late afternoon as I plodded in from one of the side fields, I noticed that Alma wasn't sitting and crocheting or knitting, as she typically did, under the massive oak tree situated in front of our house. I didn't think much of it as I walked around the back of the house towards the large kitchen window that looked out onto my mother's lovely rose garden. Since her death, I had lovingly tended to this treasure of Mother's. I found that I felt happiness and peace, just as she had, when I looked out at the flowers while working in the kitchen. The rows and rows of beautiful roses were forever creating an ocean of color. Pink, red, yellow, white, peach, and even purple all blended into a fragrant offering of beauty that could catch your breath. The potent aroma of the roses always triggered happy memories of dear Mother and her love for us children.

That is why no matter how hard I try to compose words to express my feelings, I cannot adequately describe the horror, anger, and grief that I felt at that exact moment when I saw what my stepmother was doing. There she stood yanking one of the precious rose bushes up out of the black ground and roughly throwing it down beside her. Alma's delicate, white hands were covered with work gloves, and some sharp clippers and a dirty shovel lay on the ground beside her. Other murdered rose bushes also lay scattered about. I was mortified. I couldn't comprehend what I was beholding. Alma knew that the rose garden was my mother's earthly treasure. She had yelled at me more than once to "get in here and fix my hair," "scrub the floor," "finish hanging out the clothes" when I had deviated from my work schedule to tend to Mother's roses. I had listened and followed her commands but only after stating that I would get to her after I was "done with my mother's flower garden." I would then finish watering, fertilizing, weeding, or whatever else was necessary to ensure that the beloved roses remained radiant and stunning before begrudgingly obeying Alma's orders. Could she really be right there in front of me daringly and viciously destroying Mother's defenseless creation? I was briefly frozen with shock. I could hear nothing but the blood pounding in my ears. Boom. Boom. Boom. Alma looked right at me. Her dead eyes bore into mine, and I saw the sides of her tight mouth quickly pull up into the evilest smile.

The next thing I knew, I was sprinting towards Alma with my fists clenched screaming, "You bitch! You bitch! How could you?" Her image blurred before me, and I realized that I was loudly sobbing, tears rolling unimpeded down my hot cheeks. Alma had the wisdom to run towards the outhouse and lock herself inside because she knew that at that moment, I wanted to kill her. Once I reached the devastated roses, I immediately dropped down onto my shaking knees, grabbed the first rose bush victim that I saw, and shoved its exposed, wounded roots back into one of the ugly holes in the earth. I held the main stem up with one hand while using my other hand to fill in the open space around its roots with moist, black dirt. I was trying desperately to refurbish that rose bush's life. It had to live, and I had to be the one to save it! I realized how tight my grip was on the thorny stem when I saw my own red blood dripping down it to match the color of the bush's dark, crimson roses.

I have to give her credit. My stepmother was really quite clever. It soon became apparent that she had planned this all along. My Aunt Alma, who was now my stepmother, wanted me gone for good and orchestrated the best way to make that happen. She used the destruction of Mother's roses as a crucible, and I emerged from the fire screaming the word "bitch" just as she had anticipated, thus sealing my own fate. Then all she had to do was whine, cry, yell, and relentlessly scold my father about Schlechta Wanda. Alma was either in his face screaming at him or completely ignoring him, not even allowing him anywhere near her. On and on, seemingly endlessly, she whined and complained about me.

One late afternoon I was down in the cool basement cleaning and had left the door open. Above me, I could hear Alma telling my father all kinds of hurtful lies about me since the actual truth about how bad I was didn't seem to be succeeding. The old me would have stormed up the stairs yelling and defending myself. But the new, more broken me just continued cleaning while weeping silently. I was too tired to fight. There was just so much physical work along with the pitiless, emotional and mental work of living with Alma and Father. It was never ending, and I felt like a wild horse that they were close to breaking. It wasn't long before I heard Alma give the threatening ultimatum that she had foreseen from the beginning. "Only one of us can stay here John. Is it Schlechta Wanda or is it me?"

It would be a lie to say that it barely stung my heart when he immediately picked her. Was I surprised that he picked Alma over me? No, I was not surprised; and yet, I was deeply wounded. My despair was because I recognized that the last, stubborn flicker of hope left within me had been obliterated. Before Father picked Alma, I still possessed a childlike expectancy that perhaps he really did love me after all and that he was sorry for everything that he had done and left undone. I would have forgiven him right then and there like the Bible says, "Forgiving one another just as God through Christ Jesus forgives you," if only he had chosen me. But he did not. My father, my own flesh and blood, who I had worked like a dog for my entire life, chose my stepmother. Why? I believe he did it in order to have a moment's peace from her as well as to avoid what he perceived as the absolute shame of her walking out and leaving him all alone.

On the evening of Alma's ultimate threat, Martha, Albert, and I headed out towards the cow pasture to look up at the glowing, crescent moon and splattering of stars. "I don't want you to go," cried Martha. "Damn her! I hate Alma!" A tirade of swear words spewed from her mouth.

"Martha, you really shouldn't cuss," I stated half-heartedly, knowing full well that I was a hypocrite needing to heed my own advice when it came to expletives.

Albert stood next to us uncomfortably shifting his weight from one foot to the other. I looked at Martha and remembered how heartbroken I had been when my oldest brother, Gus, left the farm to go work in Philadelphia. I knew that Martha would miss me terribly. She would cry just as she had when Paula, Richard, and Bill each left. I knew that strong, aloof, secretly sweet Albert would want to comfort her but would be unable to adequately do so.

I stood in between my younger siblings, grasping one of Martha's hands in my left hand and Albert's in my right. I squeezed gently for several moments as we all looked straight ahead into the silence of the star-filled night. "I love you both, and the Lord will provide," I finally said. There was nothing more to say. We all turned around dejectedly and walked slowly back to the house.

It was only one day later that Father drove me to Philadelphia in the middle of a severe thunderstorm, handed me fifteen dollars, and dumped me off unannounced down the street from the home of my older brother Bill and his wife, Olga. I was barely eighteen years old. He said nothing and neither did I.

PHOTOS

Konschak Farm Scenes

The building on the right side of the above picture is the home the family lived in when they moved to Hartly in 1919.
When their new home was completed, the old house was converted into a barn with a silo, as seen above.

The picture at right center is Emma and Albert in the field.

Theresa Konschak (Wanda's grandmother)

Konschak family photo
(L to R) Theresa Konschak, John Jr., Pauline Zarbok Konschak holding Jule, Gus, John Konschak with Otto standing in front of him (1906).

(L to R) Emma, Richard, Albert, Wanda, and Paula Konschak

Konschak get together—John Konschak wearing overalls, Pauline Konschak holding baby Martha, and Wanda sitting third from the right.

(L to R) Martha, Janice Hintz, Doris Hintz, Wanda, Matilda, Emma K. Hintz

(L to R) Martha, Jule, Wanda, John, Paula, and Emma Konschak

(L to R) Unknown, Albert Hintz, Edmund Hintz, Albert Konschak, Nancy and Linda Konschak on the Konschak farm

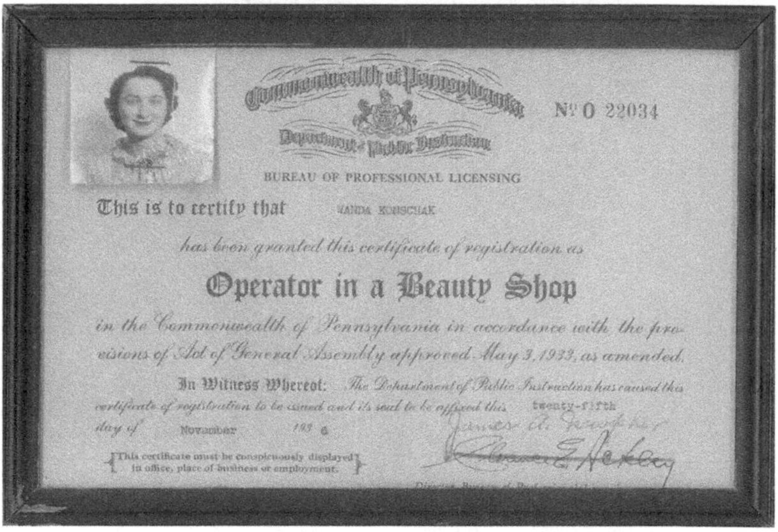

Commonwealth of Pennsylvania

No 0 22034

Department of Public Instruction

BUREAU OF PROFESSIONAL LICENSING

This is to certify that WANDA KONSCHAK

has been granted this certificate of registration as

Operator in a Beauty Shop

in the Commonwealth of Pennsylvania in accordance with the provisions of Act of General Assembly approved May 3, 1933, as amended.

In Witness Whereof: The Department of Public Instruction has caused this certificate of registration to be issued and its seal to be affixed this twenty-fifth day of November 1936

[This certificate must be conspicuously displayed in office, place of business or employment.]

Wanda's 1936 license to operate in a beauty shop.

(Center backrow) Wanda at work in the beauty shop where she met Walter.

Wanda

Wanda and Walter on a date

(L to R) Martha, Walter, and Wanda at the Jersey Shore

Walter and Wanda

Irene Belinsky (Walter's sister)

Wanda and Walter's wedding picture

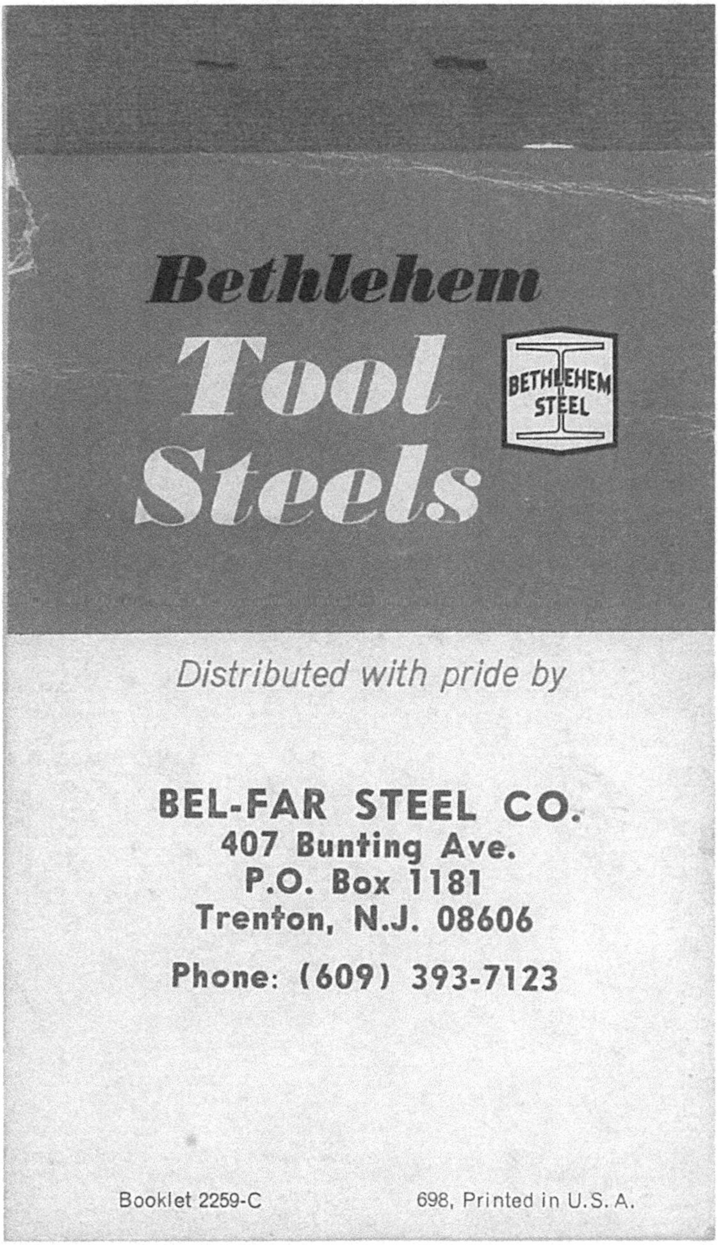

Notepad from Walter Belinsky's Bel-Far Steel company

Alma Konschak (Wanda's stepmother) grimacing,
and Wanda looking off into the distance.

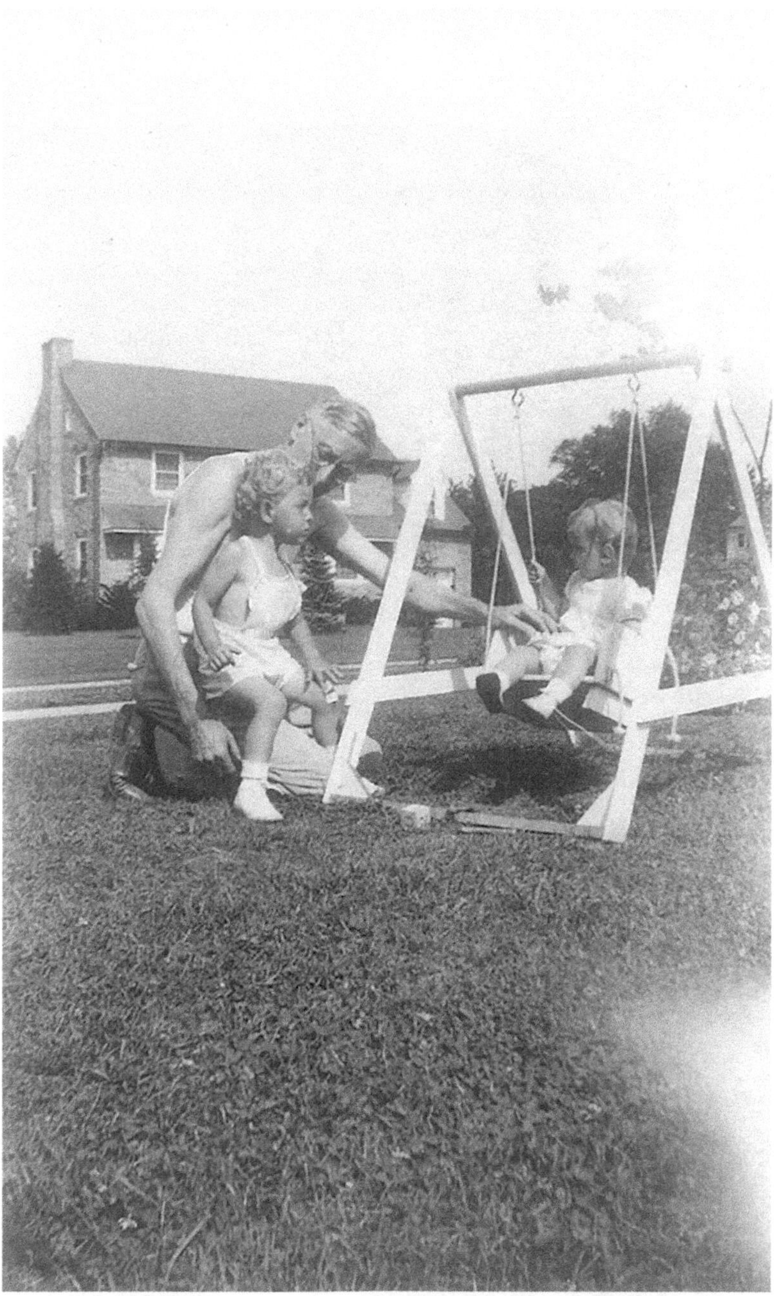

Poppy Faber kneeling with Judy and Dee-Dee on the swing.

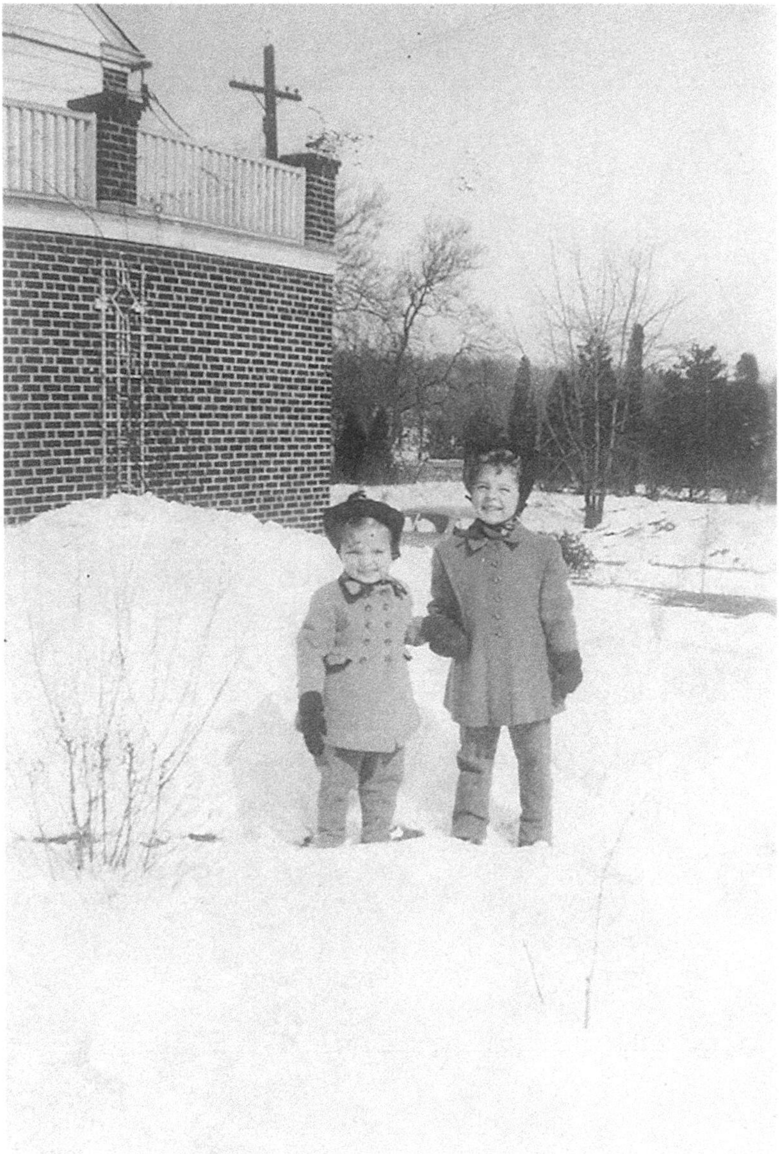

Dee-Dee and Judy posing in the backyard of their house on Leon Street.

Dee-Dee (sticking out her tongue) and Judy

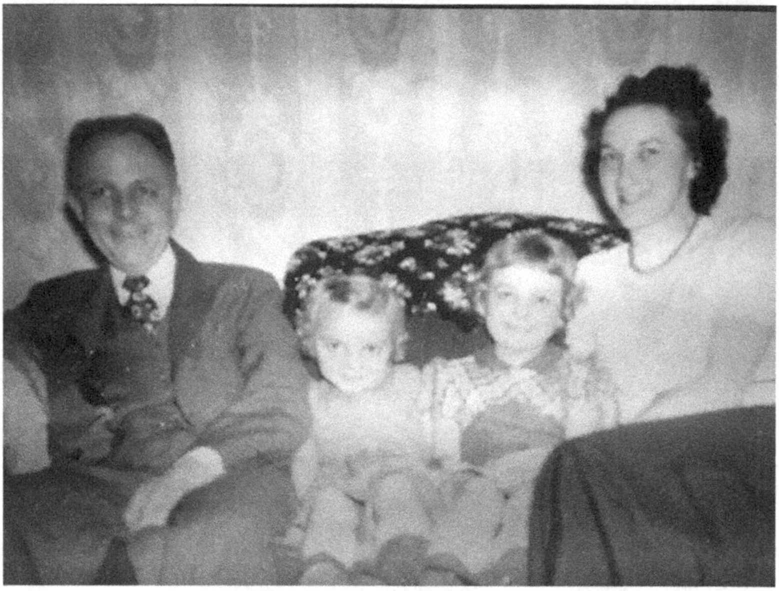

Walter, Dee-Dee, Judy, and Wanda

Judy and Dee in high school

(L to R) Kathi, Jodi, and Jeanene Glander with Wanda—notice she's wrinkle free—and Walter.

Wanda, Lydia Rose Stogner, and Kathi G. Stogner

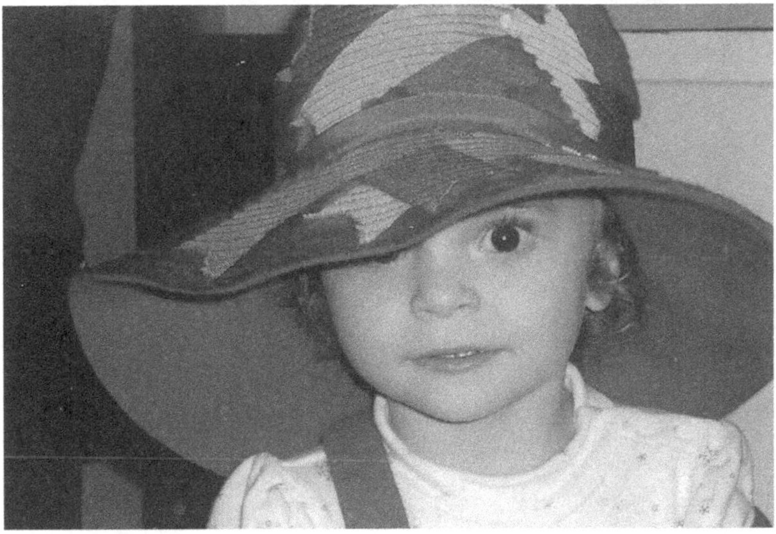

Jessica (Jessi) Stogner wearing one of Wanda's hats.

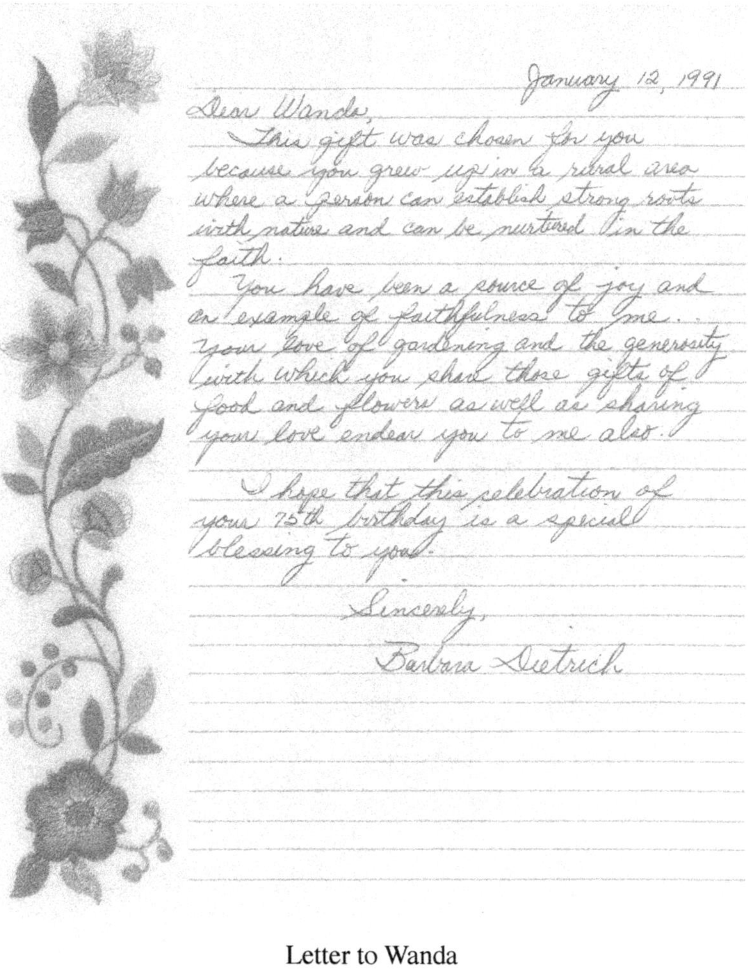

January 12, 1991

Dear Wanda,

This gift was chosen for you because you grew up in a rural area where a person can establish strong roots with nature and can be nurtured in the faith.

You have been a source of joy and an example of faithfulness to me. Your love of gardening and the generosity with which you share those gifts of food and flowers as well as sharing your love endear you to me also.

I hope that this celebration of your 75th birthday is a special blessing to you.

Sincerely,

Barbara Dietrich

Letter to Wanda

January, 1991

Dear Wanda,

Both George and I have fond memories of times spent with you - picking strawberries with both you and Walt at Styers, all the years of playing cards with both of you, Ann and Mahlon and Marion and John.

Remember working on Redeemer's PALS, LCA on their Hospitality and Property committees and of course all our ongoing projects for Redeemer"s Ladies Guild and now the Redeemer Women. And of course The Mayfairers and all the fun we used to have on their trips. I am enclosing the only good picture I have of you which was taken in 1977 while we were to Brickmann's. I still wear the shirt which George and Walt won for shufflboard.

I especially remember your kindness to me when I first joined Redeemer's Ladies Guild (about 1951 I think). At first you picked me up for meetings and encouraged me to drive myself. I did have a license which I kept renewing, but hadn't driven for over 10 years. I'm so glad today that I do drive somewhat, now that George is unable to do much.

We both wish you God's special blessings and that He will abide with you day by day.

Lovingly,
George & Eleanor

Letter to Wanda from Eleanor (friend Wanda encouraged to drive)

Mrs Belinsky:

I have fond memories of the times, when as a young girl, I would accompany my Mother to "the big house across the street from the golf course." You would cut my Mother's hair. You always had that big, bright, beautiful smile.

I also remember the spring time day we went to your home to pick-up a bike for me. That bike was special to me.

Letter to Wanda

Dear Wanda,

It's not often that people will go to a friend and tell her how they feel about her! But this is an appropriate time for me to tell you how much your friendship has meant to me over the years.

I remember so well how you used to cut my hair - for free! And remember when you gave David his first hair-cut when he was one year old - cut off his curls? The kids still speak of the fun they had sledding down the hill by your house. You gave me some slips of Coleus years ago and I still root it and plant it each spring - wonder how many years that's been? Your "green thumb" always amazed me. I also appreciate your faithfulness, hard work and dependability to the Ladies Guild over the years.

Thanks for being you, Wanda, and God bless you!

Love,
Katheryn

Letter to Wanda

Wanda and Walter's great-grandchildren/Judy and Pastor Paul Wargo's grandchildren (L to R) Michael Wargo, Trevor Capoferi, Natalie Wargo, Drew Capoferi, Owen Capoferi, Autumn Wargo, Tai Wargo, Keecie Wargo, Kendall Wargo, and Justin Capoferi

Wanda and Walter's great-grandchildren/Dee and Pastor Jim Glander's grandchildren (L to R) Lydia Stogner, Mikala Waldermo, Dee and Jim in back, Madison Waldermo and Bria Jones in front, Jessi Stogner, and Hannah Jones

Konschak farmhouse as it stands today.

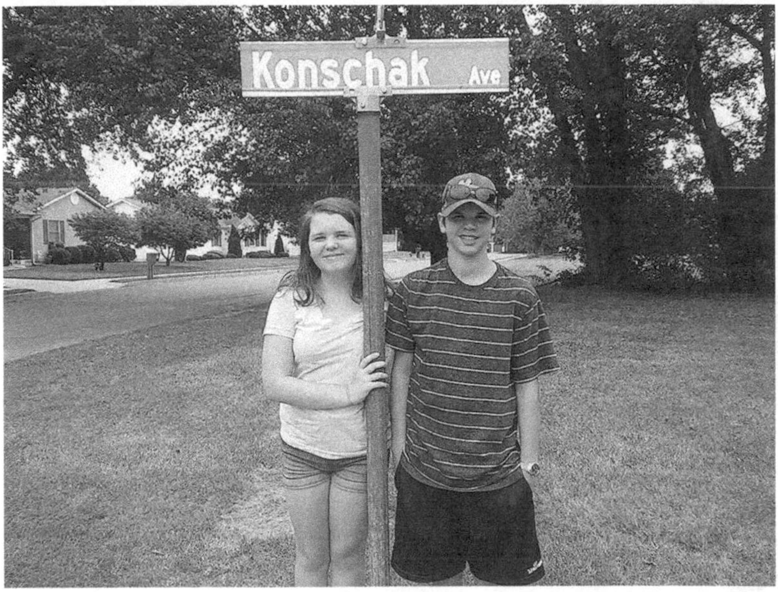

Madison and Gavin Konschak (great-grandchildren of Richard Konschak) with the Konschak Avenue street sign

One of the last pictures of Wanda K. Belinsky before her death.

INTERLUDE

THE UNBREAKABLE BOND OF THE KONSCHAK KIDS

The single most devastating event of my life, my mother's death, when combined with my banishment from the only home I ever knew, left my emotions too raw to share in any comprehensible way for a long time. I never liked to talk about the really bad things, and there are some matters that I probably won't ever tell, but I've decided that the rest of my story needs to be told, and I am going to tell it. But before I go on, I really need people to understand the strong and significant bond between my brothers and sisters and me. We always had mutual respect and love for each other because only someone who lived through the same experiences could really understand what being a Konschak was truly like and could fully acknowledge who we were. Perhaps I could best explain it by saying that my siblings were the people who clung to the shipwreck with me while we were all dragged out to sea. If it weren't for them, I may have chosen to let go of the ruins and to allow myself to drown. Thank God for my brothers and sisters. They were a continual blessing to me throughout my life. There was sometimes fierce bickering between us, but there always remained a forever lasting and unbreakable love.

Gus

My oldest brother Gus was a kind and protective older brother. I admired him and couldn't understand how he and my father could be so different. Gus was very close to our younger Hantwerker cousins who had lived near us in Marydel from 1906 to 1915 before they moved to Philadelphia. When Gus turned twenty-one, he left our farm to search for work in Philadelphia. He stayed with the Hantwerker cousins and found a job in a busy linoleum mill. I felt strangely lonely when he left. I missed talking and joking with him, and I missed him actually listening to what I had to say. Gus wrote me that he used his first paycheck to buy dress clothes so that he could go to St. Matthew's Lutheran Church in Philadelphia. I was so proud of him.

It wasn't long until Gus's mill job ended up being physically detrimental to him. I got extremely worried when every time he wrote to me, he talked about how poorly he was feeling. It turns out that while working at the mill, Gus was exposed to tremendously hazardous chemicals that quickly destroyed his health. The city doctor told him that he should stop working in the linoleum facility immediately. That was why Gus moved back to Delaware and bought thirteen acres of land on Wyoming Avenue in Dover where he could raise his own chickens. Soon after returning to Delaware, Gus went to visit my sisters Emma and Julia who still lived in Philadelphia. It was then that he met Matilda Berger—his future, spirited, blue-eyed bride. She had just recently emigrated from Germany, and the two of them could communicate in both German and English depending on who might be listening nearby. On August 10, 1927, Gus and Matilda were the first couple to be married in the new St. John's Evangelical Lutheran Church in Dover. Jule was a witness to the ceremony, and Martha was their adorable flower girl.

Later in the day, my parents hosted a large wedding dinner at our farm. I was thankful for Gus's happiness as well as for my own since it appeared that he would be living permanently in Dover, which was a lot closer to me then Philly.

Matilda and Gus were never able to have children and focused all their attention on farming and on investing in stocks. They ended up owning a large amount of land that they slowly sold off to housing developers who created neighborhoods full of new homes. Gus and Matilda even acquired a second home in Florida that they thoroughly enjoyed and always had open for visits from family and friends.

Johnny

My second oldest brother was John Jr., who we all usually called "Johnny." He was a mild-mannered and gentle person, which was definitely a liability when it came to surviving life on the farm. Johnny was born in 1903, Otto in 1904, and Julia in 1905. I figure that Johnny probably didn't get much attention since my mother had three little ones so close together. He was always very self-sufficient and independent as a result. When he and Gus started school in America, they couldn't speak English, only German. Gus learned quickly, but Johnny struggled and was very slow to pick up the English language. Father decided that Johnny would be kept home, where he stayed for the rest of his life. It was sad really because he was never given a true chance to learn in school or to be helped academically. Johnny desperately wanted schooling and would have tried so hard. When he was an adult, and could get all of his farm work done more quickly, he could be seen sitting with an open book every night. He practiced and practiced his reading with the hope of becoming better. It made me proud of him while also breaking my heart. My brother Bill said that "Johnny worked harder than anyone." It was true that Johnny was a dedicated and selfless worker. He fed the chickens, the cows, and the horses daily along with many other chores. The only main chore that Johnny didn't or couldn't do was milk the cows. I don't know if he or my father made that decision, but milking is the only thing I never saw him do.

Johnny was the first one to volunteer to stay and watch over the farm when we went to church or wanted to do any other activities. Our church had a large and very active youth group that did many things together, including playing volleyball and other sports as well as numerous, silly games. I remember being on the winning team of the bucket race many times. We had to run while carrying a bucket of water on our heads in order to win the honor of being the fastest team with the least water spilled. Girls were allowed to put rags or towels on their heads to keep their hair from getting wet, but I never needed to do that. This is the one game that Martha would never play because no one or nothing messed with her hair after I had meticulously fixed it for her. These youth group times were carefree and gave me hope. The truth is that Albert, Martha, and I were only able to attend these activities because Johnny would take care of our farm responsibilities for us while we were gone. He was a truly selfless person.

Going to dances is another of the few, truly happy memories that I have of growing up, and again, Johnny was the one who made it possible for us. I could forget about my rote life for a few hours as I danced, laughed, and intellectually conversed with people. These joyous memories I owe entirely to Johnny. Albert and Martha loved going to dances too and were both excellent and well-sought-after dance partners. I can clearly see how the Lord worked such good out of Johnny's blessing to us because Albert and Martha both ended up meeting their future spouses at dance halls.

Later in life, John Jr. had saved enough money to buy a car. He traded in our well used, unimpressive, family car and purchased a brand new, beautiful Ford. He actually had a license, but no one let him drive because we were afraid he would kill himself. Let's just nicely say that he wasn't a very good driver. The rest of us then had a magnificent, new car that Johnny had paid for but couldn't drive. He would look at the rest of us sadly but never complained when everybody else drove his car whenever they felt like it. I sure was nothing like Johnny in that respect. The first sibling that would have gotten into my car and driven it without my permission and then dared to look over at me and smile would soon have suffered from a much deserved busted lip.

It is heartbreaking to recount, but I want you to know that soft-spoken, good-tempered John Jr. suddenly became violent in 1938. I wasn't there, so thankfully I don't have any sordid details to share. All I know is that after this personality change, Father had Johnny hospitalized for a short time at an institution in Farnhurst near Wilmington, Delaware. I have no idea what they did to him or with him there as far as "treatment," and I'd rather not know. Tragically, but perhaps not surprisingly, dearest Johnny died soon after being in that institution. Whether his death was a result of his being there or whether he succumbed to pneumonia or tuberculosis (as some of my siblings believed), I still felt guilty that there was nothing I could do to save him. Another vast and ugly void had opened up in my life, and another kind person I loved was no more.

Jule

This brings me to my sister Julia or Jule, who was the oldest daughter in the Konschak clan. She was stunningly beautiful and a very bright woman with much wisdom. Like me, she had to leave school after the eighth grade to help at home with the growing family. I admired Jule, and like many younger sisters, I wanted to emulate my big sis. When Jule was eighteen or nineteen and my sister Emma was only about fifteen, the two of them bravely and happily left Delaware and the farm. They went to Philadelphia and shared a small room in a boarding house. Jule obtained a job as a housekeeper and cook for a wealthy Jewish family. Emma found work at a hosiery mill; some of the Hantwerker cousins worked there too. I was glad to hear that eventually Jule was also able to get a job at the same hosiery mill; still, the palpable absence of my much adored, older sisters wore on me like waves against the shoreline, reducing me bit by bit even though I tried to be happy for them.

Through church friends, my older sisters met and quickly fell in love with the very charismatic Hintz brothers, Edmund (Jip) and Albert (Pappy). In 1928, Jule married Jip and Emma married Pappy. I thought that it was ironic that they were both married now but still had the same last name. They just went from Konschak to Hintz. I foolishly expected both of them to ride off into the sunset like the heroines in *Jane Eyre* and *Pride and Prejudice* eventually did, but that most certainly did not happen. Each one of my sisters experienced grievous hardships but somehow never lost her faith in God.

When Jule and Jip were first married, they both really wanted to purchase a home. Jip bravely asked my father if they could borrow some money. He agreed to give them a loan but at a very high interest rate. Jule said it was "because he was a very tough German," but I told her it was "because he was a very big jerk." She laughed and went about her business without uttering a mean word.

It was tragic when Jip Hintz died at a young age, passing away in 1943. No one seemed to know for sure what caused his death. Was it pneumonia, bleeding ulcers, some hidden ailment or weakness? Sadly, this left Jule to raise their three lovely children—Edward, Janice, and Elaine—on her own. As if that wasn't bad enough, Jule developed epilepsy that same year. For four very long and anxiety ridden years, she suffered from grand mal seizures that eventually subsided to petit mal seizures. The seizures were a terrifying ordeal for Jule and for her children who relied completely on their mother to be their sole provider and caretaker. Although her illness was limiting, every Sunday Julia and her children rode the bus to Castor Gardens Lutheran Church. Jule was even able to serve as a member of the Ladies Guild there because our sister Martha accompanied her to meetings. The bus trips ended when Martha got a car and happily chauffeured them to church. Every time that I visited Jule, Edward, Elaine, and my beloved goddaughter Janice, it was obvious that while my sister and her children may have been poor in material things, they were rich in Christian heritage, faith, and love. I enjoyed spending time with them and always took my role as godmother to Janice very seriously, making sure to be both encouraging and supportive. It was so important to me that Janice knew that she was special and loved because she was indeed. I continued to look up to my big sis Jule who throughout a difficult life was always faithful to Jesus and to her family. It was a wonder and a blessing that she always kept her sense of humor and her contagious laugh. Jule was indeed a jewel. "Who can find a virtuous woman? For her worth is far above rubies" (Proverbs 31:10 KJV).

Bill

My big brother William (Bill) Konschak was born in Philadelphia on January 17, 1907. Shortly after his birth, my family moved to Marydel, Delaware. His toilsome work on the farm included anything and everything. Bill's main chore was taking care of the machines and the electric plant for the farmhouse, chicken houses, and water pump. He was essential to the proper functioning of the farm. He also ran the combine, planted corn, and shocked wheat. As I mentioned earlier, our school in Hartly that Bill was planning to attend for eighth grade mysteriously burned down; so unfortunately, his academic education ended with the seventh grade, which suited my father just fine.

I remember that Bill loved the first car our family owned. It was a sharp Model T purchased by our father for $400. Bill taught Father and attempted to teach Johnny how to drive it. Bill drove family members around even before acquiring his own drivers license. But that car, and even the newer model that Johnny later traded it in for, couldn't keep Bill on the farm. When he turned twenty-one, Bill eagerly left home to go live in the city with Emma and Jule on Clearfield Street in Kensington. He, too, worked in a hosiery mill in Philadelphia and then in hosiery mills across Delaware in the cities of Dover, Greenwood, and Wyoming before he started farming for himself. Bill met Olga Guse at our Hartly farm through the friendship between our father and Olga's father, Ewald Guse. My father and Ewald had been friends in Poland and continued their close friendship in America. Bill and Olga joyfully married in 1932 at her parents' home on Wyoming Avenue. They first lived in Philadelphia; then, in 1942, they moved to Dover where Bill started working on the Guse farm. Bill also earned money and stayed busy by working another farm on South

State Street. After much hard work, he was finally able to save enough money to purchase his in-laws' farm, also called Magnolia farm, in 1960.

Bill and Olga had two children, Gene and Bob, a girl and boy respectively. Bill asked me to be Gene's godmother, and I happily agreed. He and Olga were attentive parents who were always very active and dedicated church members, serving in all capacities at their church. I have fond memories of visiting my older brother Bill and enjoying Olga's tasty suppers while we all loudly conversed and shared stories. Laughter and smiles would fill up the day and go into the night making it difficult to say goodbye.

Baby Girl

There was also a "baby girl" Konschak who was born two months premature one cold winter and didn't survive. Mother was loading up a wagon with items to be sold in town when she slipped on the treacherous ice. She fell hard on her stomach and went into painful labor a few hours later. My sister only lived on this Earth a few minutes before her strained breathing ceased. If she had a name, only my mother knew it, and she never spoke of it to any of us. Had the baby lived, she would have grown up between Bill and Emma and would have been another one of my older sisters. I sometimes wondered how she would have looked as an adult and what kind of unique personality she would have had if her precious life had continued in this world. Like all the rest of us, this earthly place was truly not her home, and she went quickly to her heavenly one.

Emma

My sister Emma and her husband, Pappy, had one daughter, Doris, who was born in 1931 when the Great Depression was in full swing. The Depression was such a terrible hardship for so many. We were lucky on the farm because we always had food. But I do remember the sick feeling in the pit of my stomach when the huge truck would drive back up our road and dump its whole contents of our tomatoes into a gigantic pile to rot in the fields. This was because no one had money to buy them. While I was nauseous over the waste of so much effort and time, I was mainly terrified of Father's fury in losing money again. Someone would have to *pay* and that someone would be one of his kids. Emma escaped that since she was no longer living under Father's roof, but she had plenty of problems of her own. She diligently worked at the hosiery job, while Pappy could only hold a job every now and again. There was some talk that his affinity to alcohol was the culprit. Pappy had been a glazier, but during the Depression years, there was very little construction taking place. This made Pappy's trade of cutting, installing, and removing glass mostly useless. Then poor Emma contracted tuberculosis (TB) and was forced to go back to the farm in Hartly to rest. She took it easy for a few months and patiently waited to finally be accepted into the Brandywine Sanitarium, a facility that specialized in treating TB.

Little Doris was only fifteen months old when Emma went to Brandywine in 1932. I know that it broke my sweet sister's heart to be separated from her much adored child. Meanwhile, since Emma could no longer work, she and Pappy lost their home in the Mayfair section of Philadelphia. Pappy remained positive and cheerful even when he and baby Doris had to move in with his parents and four siblings: Poke, Henry, Betty, and Elsie. He found odd jobs in order to pay their room and board. One of Pappy's jobs was with our brother Bill. Pappy would drive to Hartly, and he and Bill would load up the car with fruits, vegetables, eggs, chickens, and milk before driving back to Philly to sell their wares. Because my father had always been about the money, I wasn't surprised when Bill told me, "Pop gets the largest share, but Pappy and I get our share too."

Pitiful Emma spent years in the sanitarium teetering between life and death. Miraculously, she was finally able to leave Brandywine but not until 1938. By that time, Doris was going into the second grade, and Emma had suffered so much and missed so many memory making years with her only child and her husband. I visited Emma in the sanitarium as often as was possible, but there was no way for me to ease her agonizing yearning for her daughter. I firmly believe that it was only through the power of prayer and God's provision that Emma didn't die and was able to reclaim her life with her loving family. In 1950, Emma and Pappy moved to a farm in Hartly where she busied herself with smocking, crocheting, sewing, knitting, cooking, gardening, and canning preserves. Emma was always smiling then, and I never had to ask her why.

Paula

Paula, as in my "Ode to Paula" sister, was born on May 10, 1912, on our farm in Marydel. After eventually being forced to drop out of high school to help our sick mother, Paula remained on the farm until she turned eighteen. Mother really wanted Paula to go to Philadelphia where my sisters Jule and Emma were living. She figured it would be less difficult and more exciting for Paula to begin a new life in the city than to continue working on the farm indefinitely. Paula jumped at the chance to be free, so she left and began working for a wealthy family in Elkins Park, Pennsylvania. Soon after obtaining her job, Paula joined St. Matthew's Lutheran Church. She wrote to me about how friendly the church members were, just like back at home, and I wrote to her about how very much I missed talking to her during the trip to and from church service.

For about four years, Paula cooked, cleaned, and did other chores for her rich employers. She would also accompany them every summer to the Jersey Shore, either at Margate or Vector City, which must have been so thrilling! Paula was getting paid to do the same work she would have had to do for free on our farm and was even able to go on vacations for the first time in her life. I told her that she was extremely lucky to be able to live the cliché of having her cake and eating it too. Her reply was "Wanda, life is like flying in a dream and suddenly plummeting to the ground. At some point, you will gratefully realize that you didn't die; instead, you are now fully alive." I immaturely rolled my eyes at her after that ridiculous comment and burst out laughing uncontrollably because, at that time, I had no earthly idea what in the world she was talking about. One day I would.

Paula later moved in with our brother Bill and his wife, Olga, while they still lived in a house on Orthodox Street in Philadelphia. She then had the opportunity to begin working at McCrory's 5 & 10 Cent Store as a sales girl in the glass department, which she completely loved. When Bill and Olga moved to another home, Paula remained, and Richard, Martha, and I all happily joined her. It was wonderful for the four of us to be together again even if it was only for a short time. I especially savored the added benefit of not being under Father's stern glare. The particular pain of being banished from the farm was still very fresh and raw inside of me, and I didn't need any reminders of the abuse I'd suffered up to that point. Much in the same way that I am doing it again now, I decided back then to focus on the good in my life and to leave the sordid details of how I ended up in Philadelphia for another time.

After Paula had attended St. Matthew's Church for about four years, she and her friend Agnes Hinger started selling the *Walther League Messenger* periodical for the Missouri Synod's national youth organization. They visited the houses of all the people from their church. One bright Sunday afternoon, they went to the Bergmann home and sold them the magazine. It was there that Paula met John Bergmann, who belonged to St. Matthew but never attended. After that lucky first meeting, John eagerly came to church every Sunday, and the two of them started dating. John and Paula were married at St. Matthews on November 5, 1938, and moved to 581 E. Godfrey Avenue in Philly. They had three precious children together: Paula, John, and Lois. I was so pleased to see them all cheerfully content within their family of five. Since I also ended up permanently living in Philadelphia, Paula and I were able to visit with each other quite often over the years and enjoyed countless conversations brimming with gossip and secrets.

Richard

The next in the long line of Konschak children and only about two years older than I was my brother Richard. He was born on January 18, 1914. We always had a very competitive relationship and were always trying to outdo each other. I never liked any of his girlfriends, and he always hated all of my boyfriends. I distinctly remember one day when I was eleven years old. Like a crazy dullard, I made a bet with Richard that I could fill more of the thirty-five pound baskets of tomatoes in one day of picking than he could. He seemed to mull his chances over in his head and then winked at me. He was probably picturing the fourteen acres of tomatoes with the road in the middle for a wagon or vehicle to go through and pick up the baskets left roadside. He laughed heartily and said, "You will never win," so the bet was on. To Richard's chagrin, by the end of the back-breaking day, I had picked 102 baskets of tomatoes, and he had only picked one hundred. He didn't say a word but slowly shook his head back and forth in disbelief.

"Told you I could fill more baskets of tomatoes then you," I taunted as I walked away to bask in the exhausted, sweaty glory of my painfully achieved victory. I had gotten him so good, especially since I was a girl—a younger girl at that. Crazily, I couldn't wait to do it again. The masochist in me clearly wanted to win and to be the best no matter what pain and suffering I brought to myself in the process. It is only now, in hindsight, that I can see how my determination was a blessing, but my stubborn inflexibility was (more often than not) a curse.

I also recall that after Mother died, Richard seemed more and more irritated by any men who showed me attention. Because he was so handsome, Richard was continually being chased after by one girl or another from nearby farms, school, or our church youth group. He had a plethora of girlfriends, but for whatever reason, he continually thrust himself into my love life (or lack thereof) to the point of argument. One morning after I'd finished making and serving breakfast and was preparing to scour the kitchen, I went outside to grab three roosters to decapitate. As I was returning to the kitchen to throw them into a mammoth pot of boiling water on the stove, I noticed our hired hand, Ted, picking up all the kitchen rugs. He was taking them outside to shake them out for me as he did most mornings before supper. Ted Krismal was a very thoughtful and helpful man who lived with us. There were eight boys and one girl in his family, so his parents let the oldest three sons go out and get hired as workers on neighboring farms. I thought that was quite generous of them; Ted's parents were enabling him to get a jump on life by giving him an opportunity to save up his own money. It was a lofty concept that I admired. Ted was always very kind to me, mainly by being helpful without being asked. Shaking out the dusty rugs was just one such helpful gesture. "Thanks Ted. I really appreciate you doing that for me," I said.

"No problem Wanda. It is my pleasure. Have a good morning and I'll see you at supper," Ted answered as he headed back towards the fields.

Richard had come onto the porch at the tail end of our conversation and rumpled his attractive face in disgust. Once Ted was out of hearing distance, Richard barked, "Wanda! Stop flirting with Ted. Leave him be. He's got work to do, and you're holding him up!" Richard mumbled something else under his breath letting me know that he wasn't done fussing.

"I am doing no such thing, you big bum!" I snapped back. "If you are so worried about it, why don't you do something to help me like Ted does?" I quipped, while balling up my fists. It seemed like a completely valid question to me. Richard was jealous of Ted helping me, but he definitely didn't step in to offer assistance. "Thank God I've got a stranger here who's doing for me!" I added.

"Ahhhh, dammit Wanda! Just stop!" Richard ordered.

I wanted to ask him exactly what it was that I was supposed to stop since I wasn't doing anything, but instead I just calmly retorted, "Make me." It was enough to shut him up and he exited, loudly slamming the porch door behind him. In actuality, I was only seventeen, and Ted was in his twenties, which I considered to be an old man at the time. I seriously had no romantic interest in him whatsoever, but to hell with letting Richard know that. I would let him stew because that's what he got for injecting his nose into situations where he wasn't wanted.

Richard was really never very interested in farming but remained on the farm until his early twenties when he finally, eagerly left for Philadelphia. He worked in the city as a machinist for Midvale, Crown Can, Bud, and eventually Bel-Far Steel companies. At Bel-Far Steel, he ran the machines, cut steel, and made truck deliveries.

Richard continued to have numerous girlfriends until our sister Paula intervened. She introduced Richard to her dear friend Agnes Hinger in 1937, and Agnes's grandparents, the Rumpendols, also separately orchestrated a meeting. Paula was so pleased when Richard and Agnes immediately stopped dating other people and went together exclusively. I was rather shocked that Richard was so smitten with Agnes that he quickly started talking about getting married. I really liked her though. This is going to sound arrogant, but she reminded me a lot of myself, which was a good thing since I figured Richard would need a strong-willed woman to reign him in every once in a while. Richard and Agnes genuinely had a great and powerful love for each other. They, too, were married at St. Matthew's Lutheran Church in Philadelphia on the glorious day of March 8, 1941. God blessed them with two handsome sons, Robert and Walter, and one lovely daughter, Evelyn.

In 1960, Richard left the steel business and worked at Giles and Ransome in parts and maintenance. His new job was only one-and-one-half miles from his house, which gave him the opportunity to come home for lunch and to start and maintain a family garden on his half-acre lot. I suppose the desire for fresh vegetables remained in his blood and was eventually inescapable in its pull of his fingers towards the black dirt.

It was completely shocking and acutely devastating when Richard's health began to dramatically deteriorate in 1968. It was the beast, lung cancer, and he only lived until July 14 of that same year. His sudden death at the age of fifty-four was a traumatic blow to his wife and children. Not that having more time to prepare would have made his absence any easier, but its speed was dizzying and led to cruel incomprehensibility and understandable denial. I remained extremely close to Agnes and thought of her not only as a friend, but also as another one of my dear sisters. I loved spending time with her and my nephews and niece. Richard lived on for me inside of them and hopefully within me for them too.

Albert

I came next in the birth order, followed shortly thereafter by Albert in 1918 and Martha in 1920. The three of us were always very close. We quarreled and teased but also loved and helped each other survive, particularly after what happened to Mother. Albert, Martha, and I were not just emotionally strong, we were all also very physically tough and athletic. In fact, Albert and Martha were the fastest runners in our school and in our town. My specialty was dodgeball. I threw hard, and I could hit anyone and everyone while, more often than not, avoiding being hit with the dodgeball myself. My reflexes were quick and my aim deadly. Classmates were justifiably terrified of me.

Along with being a gifted runner, Albert excelled in football and baseball. He was the talk of the town when it came to athleticism, and Albert was the essential component necessary to assure victory for his team. Father would allow Albert to go and play in the home games but said he couldn't go to games that were away. Father believed that away games would take up too much of Albert's time that was supposed to be spent doing farm work. Before every occurrence of an away game, the dedicated school teacher, who was also the coach, would appear on the long road leading to our farm. He would calmly beg my Father to let Albert go to the away game. Sometimes my dictator-like father conceded, sometimes not. That poor coach came back before every single away game. The déjà vu must have been something between tortuous and exasperating for him. Almost weekly, the patient coach would arrive and the well-rehearsed pleading would begin. He understood that just because my father said Albert could go to an away game one time didn't automatically mean that he could go the next time. Again and again the coach faithfully came. I thought that it was ridiculous and mighty mean that Father made the coach come repeatedly to appeal for Albert's right to excel in sports. Albert was extremely grateful for all of the time and effort his coach put into helping him be able to compete in athletics and happily repaid Coach with win after win.

Albert and I liked to annoy each other. We got sick pleasure out of bothering one another almost daily; although, maybe I should just speak for myself and say that I had tremendous fun trying to rile up Albert. It was even worth getting a busted lip or a bruised eye. One of my simplest, yet most effective vexations of Albert came one day while he was sitting on the plow guiding the horses through the ripe earth. I took immediate notice of the look of complete and focused concentration on his face. He was deep in thought about what he was doing and, as usual, wouldn't want to be disturbed. I saw my chance and decided to take it. I picked up a random piece of yellow straw that was laying on the ground near my foot and held it between the pointer finger and the thumb on my left hand. I slowly moved my arm back and forth, back and forth, aiming it perfectly towards his focalized face. Then, boom! I released my rocket and the piece of straw went sailing right by Albert's nose almost impaling him in the eye. I was laughing so loudly that I forgot to run until Albert shot off of the seat of the plow like a bullet from a gun. I sprinted with everything in me towards the house, hoping to outrun him and knowing that if I didn't, there would be hell to pay. I dashed into the kitchen and only came to a complete stop when I stood directly in front of Mother like she was the judge and I the defendant. It was lucky for me that Albert would never do anything to me in front of her, so I knew that I was safe. I was beyond thankful that my legs were longer than Albert's and that fact, along with my older age, had helped me escape him this time. I was victorious in my effort to get him good. Fluttering my long dark eyelashes in his direction with mock innocence, I thoroughly enjoyed my triumph and reveled in it as I watched his face turn red with anger.

When Albert was twenty, he began saving money for his escape from Father by working a paying job in a hosiery mill in Wyoming, Delaware, while also continuing to labor on the farm. He wanted to finally be able to save enough money of his own to begin a life far away from our father. As I mentioned earlier, Albert loved to dance; in fact, he met his future wife, the stunning Susanne Lissy, when he daringly cut in while she danced with a friend. After dating for three years, they joyfully married in 1940 in the parlor of the Hartly farmhouse. Martha rubbed her organ and piano talents in Father's face by expertly playing Albert and Susanne's wedding music even though Father had refused to pay for her piano lessons many years before. Immediately after the invigorating wedding and joyous reception filled with lively dancing, Albert and Susanne moved to Philadelphia, and Albert worked for Bel-Far Steel. In 1941, at the strong urging of the Konschak family, they moved back to the Hartly farm. At first Albert rented and then eventually bought the entire farm from Father, who moved to a new home in Dover.

Before leaving the farm, Father held a large sale of items he no longer wanted. One of the items was an ancient clock that had been in the musty basement for years. It hadn't worked for a long while, and Albert took it upon himself to fix the antique. Albert really liked the ornate details of the attractive, newly functioning clock, so he asked Father if he could have it now that it was working properly. Father refused to give it to him saying that Albert would have to buy the clock if he wanted to keep it. Even one of our neighbors thought it unfair for Father to be so greedy and cold towards Albert. That same neighbor wanted to buy the clock just so that he could give it to Albert, but Albert talked the kind neighbor out of the purchase. He refused to accept it as a gift since his own father wouldn't give it to him when he'd asked.

Father, as always, was all about the money and wouldn't give Albert a break or monetary reprieve in any way when it came to Albert's buying the Konschak farmstead. In fact, Father even accused Albert of doing dishonest things in regards to the farm, which was a complete lie because if there was one thing Albert was, it was extremely honest. Even with my father making it so difficult (when Albert was actually doing him a favor by taking the farm off his hands) Albert was determined and still purchased the farm. Despite Father's habitual mistreatment, Albert had claimed the farm as his very own, and I was exceedingly happy for my baby brother.

Albert was extremely productive on the farm like he had always been, but now it was his own, and he could reap all the benefits. He tilled approximately 180 acres of land, raised 8,000 chickens, and milked up to forty cows twice a day. Susanne had also grown up on a farm and naturally fell into the role of a hardworking farmer's wife. Albert very rarely asked his three lovely daughters—Linda, Nancy, and Marlene—to do farm work even though they were being raised on the same large, demanding property that he had toiled on as a child. It was clear to me that Albert refused to be like our self-absorbed father who gave us no choices. Albert's children would have choices. His daughters would also have infinite chances for laughing, playing, and being carefree kids. Albert's lucky girls would even have what Albert's sisters never did—the privilege of education and of choosing their own path in life.

I will always remember Albert's love of children and his desire to have fun with them regardless of his tough outward appearance. The city kids, who came with their parents to visit the Konschak farm, all remember actually being shocked when Albert grabbed their hands while also grabbing the electric fence. The children got quite a jolt and were stunned for a few moments before it registered with them that Albert had really shocked them all. Once they understood what he'd done, they joined in with his hearty, amused laughter. Albert was also known to playfully squirt you in the face with milk if you haphazardly entered the barn during milking time. "You looked thirsty," he'd say, and the kids couldn't help but smile at his robust laughter even before having a chance to wipe the milk off of their dripping faces.

Dear Albert still had one last terrible cross to bear. In 1963, when he was only forty-five years old, Albert suffered a major stroke. It was really a miracle that he survived at all; but the Albert who did survive, although still physically strong, was only half of himself. The whole left side of Albert's body was paralyzed. He worked hard to still speak and did communicate even though the left side of his face drooped down and was immoveable like a horse with broken legs. His left arm hung useless at his side, and he dragged his left leg slightly behind him as he walked like he was unable to bend it. If he ever lost his balance and fell over, it was nearly impossible for him to get upright without assistance. Albert was a proud man, and I know it killed him to have to accept help from others. I saw his frustration demonstrated in the embarrassed expression on his red face when anyone offered assistance. Through it all, Susanne remained a faithful, hard-working, and loyal wife who deeply loved Albert with a fierceness that was inspiring to me. To see so much spitfire mixed with patience coming from such a small, beautiful woman was truly something to behold. During one visit, I told her within hearing distance of Albert, "Susanne, you are really something special to be able to put up with my brother."

"He knows when he's met his match," she replied before winking at me.

I don't know that it surprised anyone when Albert and his family remained on the farm after his stroke. Although most of the land was rented out to other farmers, Albert still grew delicious vegetables and unusually gorgeous flowers and sold his produce to passersby. He also focused on the plentiful grape vineyard, several walnut trees, and about twelve beehives. People drove for miles to buy Albert's wine and honey and commented on the beauty and efficiency of the farm. Susanne remained the proud matron of the Konschak farmhouse, and it never looked better. If you ever have a chance, you should drive down Konschak Avenue in Hartly, Delaware, and take a look. It is powerfully ironic how the same farm that brought Albert tremendous pain also flooded him with unspeakable joy and peace. By the grace of God, Albert's family and his farm saved him and gave him purpose.

Martha

The last of the John Konschak brood was Martha. She was born in the parlor of our family homestead and brought into this world by a midwife. As I mentioned earlier, being the baby only got Martha out of farm work until she was six. Martha had to get up before 4:30 a.m., like the rest of us, the very day she left the lucky land of a five-year-old. There was no going back to any days of complete fun and rest. It would forevermore be work, work, and more work.

There were three things Martha truly hated. She hated getting up out of her warm, feather bed soon after 4:00 a.m. to fly to the horrid outhouse. This was because that loathsome outhouse was absolutely freezing in the winter and full of noisy, creepy bugs in the summer. Martha also despised the extremely heavy and depleting work of having to pick bushel baskets of tomatoes. She might have even hated it more than I did. The third thing that Martha couldn't stand was messy, unkempt hair. This was particularly true if it was her own hairdo that had been wrecked. Once I had fixed Martha's hair *just so* for the day, nobody or nothing better mess it up!

I admired Martha's daring. Sometimes she and Richard would sneak away from their chores and mischievously ride the work horses. Martha always had problems with her horse though. He would take her straight to the orchard and stubbornly dump her off, or else as soon as she had started out, he would turn around and run back to the stable to finish eating his daily oats. I thought it was hilarious and couldn't keep myself from laughing every time I witnessed such comedy, but, of course, dauntless Martha didn't find it one bit funny and let me know accordingly. Martha was always very much a tomboy, and she got into numerous fights at school, mainly with unwise boys who dared to call her a "farm girl." I was always proud of how well she was able to defend herself.

Martha enjoyed the evenings. While Mother was still alive, she often climbed into Mom's warm bed and slept a while until Father made her leave. Martha also enjoyed being with our brothers. She thought that they were all quite wonderful, especially Richard. When Martha was eleven years old, Richard started sneaking her out of the house with him so that she could see her ten-year-old boyfriend. It was unfortunate that one evening Martha was met at the door by our irate father who chased her up the main stairs and back down the other set of stairs before whipping her good. Mother arrived soon after this violent confrontation to comfort the crying Martha who had hidden under her bed. Little did Martha know that before she turned thirteen, she would lose this motherly source of solace forever.

Our father made Martha drop out of high school when she was in the tenth grade. She really couldn't stand being on the farm then because almost all of her siblings were gone. She wrote to me about how terribly she missed Richard, Bill, Paula, and me. It was not too surprising when Martha ran away at the age of seventeen and came to live with Paula and me on Orthodox Street in Philadelphia. It was a blessing to once again be living with her; daily, we were able to share our highs (what we liked to call *roses*), and our lows (otherwise known as *thorns*). Martha quickly got a job at McCrory's 5 & 10 Cent Store and worked there until she turned eighteen. She then got a position at an exclusive department store called Blum's making fourteen dollars a week. Martha sold clothing and modeled gloves and shoes on her petite extremities. She loved that job and worked there until she was twenty. Her next job was working for the Budd Company in the World War II effort. She was a fast welder and one of the best there. Martha helped the other girls finish their work when they got behind and was excited to be making sixty-five dollars a week back in 1942. She was able to save quite a bit of money during that time.

When Martha was twenty, she went to La Casa Canteen dance hall where there was dancing, food, and sodas. She accompanied her best girlfriend Eileen, after whom she later named her daughter. On her third visit to La Casa, a handsome young man named Ray Karutz started dancing with her. He remarked that she was "the best dancer I have ever met." I didn't believe in such a thing, but Martha said it was love at first sight. After only two dates, the enamored Ray asked her to marry him! It was very unfortunate that they ended up having to wait four years because Ray had just used all of his money to pay off his parents' house before they lost it. He had been saving $4,000 to use to get married one day but gave it all to his parents instead. Of course, right after doing that was when he met Martha. Martha recognized that Ray was a generous man for having done such a selfless thing for his parents. She loved that he was a Christian, specifically a faithful Baptist, who went to church every Sunday. Ray worked hard as a gas station attendant for Texaco until he got a big break at the Milton Roy Chemical Company. Martha and Ray finally got married on October 21, 1944, in St. Matthew's Lutheran Church. They had their daughter, Eileen, a few years later. Ray and Martha purchased a row house in Philadelphia, and it would be nearly impossible to count the number of times Martha and I visited at each other's homes. We were so much more than sisters; we were best friends and loyal supporters of each other regardless of life's circumstances.

Part 2
LIVING IN PHILLY

Chapter 18

A FARM GIRL'S LIFE IN PHILADELPHIA

After my father chose Alma, drove me to Philadelphia, and abandoned me, it was with mixed emotions that I slowly walked across Bill's yard and towards the threshold of my oldest brother's house. Shock, sorrow, terror, excitement, anger, and anticipation mixed inside me like a powerful whirlpool and left me feeling discombobulated. "The Lord will provide," I repeated over and over to myself. I looked up and saw a magnificent rainbow stretching across the blue sky, its colors spilling into perfect arches of stunning color. It bespoke of new beginnings and gave me hope. One part of my life was over, but another new segment was just beginning to unfold. I wondered what would become of Schlechta Wanda Konschak now. I set down my lone suitcase and knocked firmly on the door.

Within a week, I had a job as a live-in housekeeper for a well-to-do family in a small neighborhood known as Frankford, which was located near the northeast section of Philadelphia. Since I hadn't unpacked my suitcase yet, it was a quick and easy move from Bill's to the Burress's home. Mr. Burress was a prominent, Jewish businessman who owned a furniture store nearby, and he and his wife had three handsome little boys. The youngest son was two-and-a-half, and Mrs. Burress immediately had his crib put into my bedroom. Every night, I tiredly awoke around midnight to go downstairs and make him a warm bottle so that he could return to sleep. Waking up in the middle of the night gave me too much time to dwell on how lonely I felt without Albert and Martha. I missed them terribly.

I did every drop of that woman's work and was constantly washing, ironing, cooking, and cleaning. When I first arrived at Mrs. Burress's house, her stove was so dirty that I couldn't stand it. That nasty stove was the very first thing that I cleaned in her very unkempt, filthy home. I was amazed that she could sit idly on her tail all day long reading a magazine, a book, or a newspaper. Maybe she was depressed, but to me she just seemed very, very lazy. She even walked lazily. It was a good thing that I lived there because she really did nothing for her family. I took excellent care of the little guy and his brothers as if they were my own. I really felt quite sorry for the children because they got scant, if any, attention from their lethargic mother.

I made ten dollars a week working there for almost a year. Then I decided to do something with my love and talent for fixing people's hair, so I enrolled in Marinella Hairdressing School. Three days a week, I would quickly do all the Burress housework, feed them, and clean up after lunch before running to beauty school. Before I knew it, the time would come for me to swiftly return to the Burress's in order to prepare an elaborate and hearty meal for their dinner. Even though I still got everything done, for my time absent, Mrs. Burress lowered my pay to seven dollars and fifty cents a week.

I didn't have much of a social life at that time except that some neighbor girls taught me to roller skate, and I faithfully went to my church's Walther League youth group activities. It felt satisfying to be earning my own money for doing work I had always done for free. I also loved finally being back in a school setting where I thrived. It was intriguing to learn about trendy, new hair styles and expert cutting and perming techniques.

Time flew by as I scrubbed, swept, ironed, babysat, cooked, studied, cut, permed, and dyed. When I first accepted the job with the Burress family, it was agreed that I would have every other Sunday off to attend church at St. Matthew's Lutheran along with Richard, Paula, and several other of my siblings. Church, with its worship and camaraderie, was still as important to me as it had always been. I told myself that some part of my father must have loved me, at least for a little while, because he was the one who first took me to church and made sure that I knew about God, Jesus, and the Holy Spirit. It was perplexing that he clearly knew how important faith in Christ was for my salvation but still couldn't make himself act like a Christian when it came to his interactions with me. I was his blind spot. All of his children were in his blind spot actually. My father's behavior towards us should have and needed to match his theology, but it certainly did not!

On one typical Sunday morning at the Burress house, I had gotten ready for Sunday school and church very early in the morning and was attempting to leave the premises. The matron kept giving me extra jobs to do before I left, completely hindering my exit. "Mix us up some chicken salad for lunch," she said. That request was really time consuming because it required me to fry up chicken breasts, boil eggs, and cut up celery, pickles, and herbs, but she clearly didn't care if I was late. "Wanda. Quick. Sweep the front porch and the steps," she added. I finally finished those tasks and was on my way out the side door with my coat and purse slung over my arm. I caught a glimpse of the Mr. and Mrs. lounging and reading the newspaper. She had her large, slippered feet propped up on the flowered sofa and pink foam curlers in her hair. I had almost escaped when I heard her loudly calling, "Wanda! Wanda! The baby has got poopy in his pants. Come back and clean it up!" The littlest guy must have recently pooped in his pants, and Mrs. Burress had smelled the stink and didn't want to have to clean him up herself. I turned around begrudgingly to respond with concurrence and saw her husband sit up abruptly before he yelled, "Wanda, you go out that door and you go to church! This is your day off!" Then he looked directly at his wife and, I hate to say, hollered at her, "You are lazy like a son of a bitch. You get up and change your own kid!" Mrs. Burress and I were both shocked. I had never ever heard him raise his voice or cuss at her before. He could have just cleaned up his son himself, and I knew that a husband should never swear at his wife, but I was still overtly relieved and secretly glad that Mr. Burress said what he did to her that day. She needed someone to slap her back into reality, as did I. After that pivotal morning, I had more guts about not working on my day off. I figured that it was my only free day during every two-week period after all. She could do her own work that one day. I was thankful that Mr. Burgess stood up for me, thus enabling me to later stand up for myself. I had pushed Schlechta Wanda so far down after Alma and my father kicked me out that it was refreshing to have my guts, pride, and voice back. I felt truly alive and fearless again.

It wasn't long after this rebirth that I was able to completely stop being a live-in housekeeper and go to beauty school full time. I was only able to do this because my sister Paula generously loaned me $250. Students had to have 1,000 hours in hairdressing school before being allowed to take the state test. Paula enabled me to get my hours in much more quickly, and I was very grateful. I didn't have a high school diploma or a college degree, but I did get a certificate of registration to be an operator in a beauty shop. The Commonwealth of Pennsylvania

Department of Public Instruction and Bureau of Professional Licensing certified me as Beautician number 22034. It was one of the happiest days of my life.

When I graduated from hairdressing school, it took me a few weeks to feel comfortable saying that I was a professional hairdresser, even though I immediately went to work for a well-known Italian hairdresser on Chestnut Street. For my whole life I had been a farm girl, the daughter of the successful farmer John Konschak. I had been Schlechta Wanda as well as a succorer and surrogate mother to my family after dear Mother had died. Now I had no one to take care of except myself and no one to struggle against or defy. It felt odd and unnatural to not have to fight a daily battle against Father, Alma, nature and the elements, boredom, physical exhaustion, or even time. I was like a boxer left in the ring without an opponent ready to bloody me. I slowly learned to relax and to enjoy the peace.

The Italian hairdresser had another girl along with me working for him. He wouldn't let us do a whole head of hair all by ourselves, but we really learned a great deal from him. I would do the shampooing and then watch intently while he pinned the pin curls flat, which is how I learned to pin them flat myself. He would eventually let us pin the curls ourselves before he combed them out. He was a phenomenal haircutter and that was what I was really interested in pursuing. He employed cutting techniques that I had never seen before.

After staying with the trendy hairdresser for a year, I decided to try to get a job working for the Edelmann sisters. They had their own beauty shop in Oxford Circle in Philadelphia. I called Edelmann's Salon to see if they would hire me. That shop was very close to where I lived with some of my siblings, which was really appealing. I also liked the fact that women owned the business and ran it successfully by themselves. I decided that I wanted to be a part of something spearheaded by strong women who would acknowledge my individual talent, passion, and strength. When I got the job, I had no idea that the entire course of my life would be changed by that one decision.

Edna Edelmann was the boss of the beauty shop. She asked me to take her customers whenever she got really busy. In fact, I did all of her regular customers that spring while she was occupied with doing time-consuming permanents. The next time the customers I'd worked on came into the shop, they asked for me instead of her. They now wanted "Wanda" to do their hair. Edna was noticeably jealous and got really mad at me even though I was only doing what she had asked me to do. I truly never intended to *steal* her customers.

I told her, "I don't want them. I really don't want them. Take them back!"

She resignedly replied, "Well, they asked for you, so I have to give them to you," and that was that. I settled into a busy and profitable routine and the days flew by.

I had been working at the Edelmann Salon for just over a year when a man named Walter Belinsky dropped off his sister one Saturday morning. The sister's name was Irene, and Edna had done her hair several times, but on that particular day, she asked me to do it. Edna wanted me to comb out Irene's hair so that she could leave work for the day. It was summertime and that meant that Edna and her sister were done at noon. The rest of us had to stay until everybody in the shop was dried and combed out, the brushes washed and sterilized, and the entire floor swept. After Irene's hair was dry, I gently combed it out. "Oh, you have the prettiest hair! You really have nice hair," I told her, because she did. This young, thin, very tall girl with absolutely beautiful blonde hair soon became one of my favorite customers. I chose to focus on her hair and our cheerful conversations while most other people simply stared at her unusual face.

Irene had been born with a cleft lip, which is a split in the top lip that makes a space between the person's lip and nose. She also had a cleft palate meaning that she had a hole in the top of her mouth where her hard palate did not fuse together correctly in the womb. The best that a doctor could do was to try and pull some of the skin under Irene's nose together and to jaggedly sow part of the visible opening shut. He left the problematic but hidden hole in her mouth alone and did nothing about her misshapen nose, which lacked symmetry and pulled down on one side. She had a very large and long chin and must have been sensitive about her somewhat misplaced teeth because she never showed them when she smiled. Sweet Irene did smile a great deal regardless of the stares, uneasy laughter, and ugly labels many people hurled in her direction. I found Irene's smile to be a truly wonderful and beautiful thing and thought her very brave.

In the near future, such a birth defect would be easily rectified with surgery that would leave only a small scar. At that time, though, plastic surgery of this sort was not readily available, even in America, so Irene went through her life being gawked at, teased, and otherwise abused by many cruel members of society. I was not one of those people! When she came into the shop, I immediately ushered her into my chair and began complimenting her on her truly beautiful hair. I never stared at her, acted shocked, or treated her differently from anyone else whom I served. We talked the entire time she was with me. She and I laughed together a great deal, and she beamed during her entire appointment. I had no idea, at that time, that I was making a huge impression on Irene. I didn't realize that she talked incessantly about "this girl called Wanda, who I am sure is Polish because Wanda is a Polish name, who is such a nice girl" to her older brother Walter. It was always this same Walter who brought her to the shop weekly and then picked her up outside after I was done fixing her hair.

Chapter 19
WALTER B. BELINSKY

John and Mary Belinsky were devout Catholics who had four children named Frank, Walter, Joseph (or Joe), and Irene. Another Belinsky son had died when he was just a toddler. They lived next door to an Irish family, and the Irish family happened to be very close friends with the Edelmanns. Their children grew up playing together, and the two families even went on vacations with each other. That is how Edna Edelmann knew the Belinsky boys and why Walter brought his sister to her shop.

Walter called Edna one afternoon asking, “How can I talk to Wanda?” Edna responded by saying she would speak to me first. The next day when I was in the shop, Edna talked to me about Walter.

“Is he Catholic?” was the first thing I asked her after she brought him up.

“Yes,” she answered.

“I don’t want to talk to him then. That’s all I’ve met since I’ve been here in Philly, and I’m not going near him,” I blurted out abruptly.

In retrospect, this sounds rather harsh, but you have to understand what it was like between Catholics and Lutherans back then. We chose not to mix. Although we were both Christians,

Catholics had their specific beliefs, rituals, and practices, and Lutherans (like myself) had ours. With all my non-farm activities always revolving around the Lutheran church and my youth group, I had no desire to have my life infiltrated by what I considered questionable Catholic dogma.

"Oh Wanda," Edna moaned. "He's a nice guy! He can take you on nice trips." She went on and on with her list of all Walter could do for me.

"I don't want that." My response was simple and to the point.

Soon after this conversation, a call came into the shop at around 11:30 on a Saturday morning. Edna indicated that the caller had asked for me and didn't tell me who it was. When I came to the phone, I found out that it was Walter. I must say that he had a wonderful telephone voice. He sounded very professional, and his voice was deep, yet kind. It projected dignity and intelligence, and I liked that. Walter explained who he was and told me all about himself including the fact that he was thirty. I thought that was a very truthful thing for him to do because I was sure that Edna had told him I was only twenty-two. He had to have known that I would think his being thirty meant that he was practically an old man. Walter ended our first conversation by simply wanting to know if he could come to the shop and escort me home. Miraculously, I let him.

The first time I actually saw Walter B. Belinsky and gave him any of my attention, I honestly thought to myself, "Oh, no!" He was not tall and I preferred tall. I found him to be short compared to most of the other men I knew. In actuality, we were close to the same height but it was obvious to me that if I'd been wearing higher heels, I would have been looking down at him. He had light blond hair that was wavy (versus curly like his sister's) and a wispy, blond mustache. I was attracted to men with thick, dark hair and dark brown eyes, so he definitely didn't catch my attention right away. Walter's eyes were hazel; they could be blue, green, or gray. I remember that they were light blue that day like the Caribbean Sea I'd once seen in a picture book. He had rosy, circular cheeks that were really accentuated whenever he smiled, as he often did. I also recall that he was impeccably neat and nicely dressed with everything about him polished and perfected, quite handsome really, if I'd been willing to admit it at the time. Walter's looks were *nice*, but I preferred muscular and tough looking not sweet and intellectual, or so I thought. That is why the first time he asked me out after taking me home from work, I immediately declined the offer. I then nicely declined numerous invitations from Walter to go on a real date. Walter was so persistent and purposeful yet so sweet about it. He never gave up, continually calling and stopping by the shop in person to inquire if I might accompany him on a date.

The main reason that I still continued to turn him down was because I knew that he was a devout Catholic. His sister and I had multiple conversations about our religion and our faith, and she and Walter knew that I was a staunch Lutheran. As I mentioned earlier, during this time, Catholics and Lutherans did not often mix or interact with each other socially, and they were especially opposed to interacting romantically. I don't know what to compare it to nowadays, perhaps a Jewish person dating a Muslim comes close. A Lutheran and a Catholic getting together in the 1930s was frowned upon in the same way that a black person and a white person being romantically linked in the 1960s was viewed with disapproval. Depending on the person you talked to back then, a Catholic and a Lutheran dating or marrying was foolhardy at best and a treasonous sin at worst.

It was strange and at first uncomfortable for me that Walter was strong in a different way than I had ever known a man to be. He was not physically strong. Walter didn't hurl heavy hay bales into a stack or use his bare hands to beat down the black earth forcing it to produce crops. He was powerful in wit, humor, intelligence, and determination. Walter was strong in his ability to show me that he could be vulnerable when it came to me, and it drew me towards him with a mixture of fascination and longing. But I was very stubborn and hard-headed, so it was quite a long period of time after my initial decision to reject him before it became obvious to me that Walter was never ever going to give up on me. He was willing to risk so much for us to be in a relationship. Instead of causing humiliation, my consistent rebuffs seemed to feed his resolve to win me over. Walter's determination to get what he wanted, along with his kindness and ability to make me laugh, weakened my defenses against him. Once I finally acknowledged all of his admirable qualities, I had no other choice but to finally agree to go out with him.

Walter overwhelmed me. He took me to dinner, theatrical productions, museums, and symphonies. We enjoyed movies, bowling, long walks, and countless hours of conversation. He spoiled me with fun day trips and quick visits to the shore. I liked how Walter eagerly introduced me to all of his friends and family members and was always the perfect gentleman. I admit that Walter treated me like a princess, and I thoroughly enjoyed it. I had never been spoiled before. I could see the pride in his eyes when others acknowledged me, and I felt more beautiful inside and out then I ever had at any other time in my life. I had always had good posture and an erect carriage, but Walter made me want to stand even taller and to push back my broad shoulders with even more confidence and ease. I loved that Walter was a God-fearing man who was extremely intelligent, hard-working, and purposeful in his life. If he said he was going to do something, he did it. Walter was committed and empowered to succeed without being haughty or cruel. He was the complete opposite of my father.

Time flew by, and before I realized it, I had gone out with Walter for almost three months. Another of the things that I really liked about him was that he didn't try to kiss me good night or to touch me in any inappropriate way. He was very different from the other boys that I had dated in Philly. They had all been pushy and intent on being physical. Some of them had learned the hard way that if I said that I didn't want them to touch me, I meant it. One jerk had even dared to raise his hand to me, obviously expecting me to shrink back and give up. In actuality, he riled me up even more and brought down upon himself the fury of Schlechta Wanda aimed specifically at his groin. The last that I saw of him, he was cursing me under his breath as he made a hasty retreat. Walter was not like the others at all. He was always very respectable. I didn't have to worry at all about him trying to have sex with me when he hadn't even kissed me. I never had to have a conversation with him about how I was not going to have sex until I was married. When I got to the point within myself that I really did want him to kiss me, it was a wonderfully new feeling.

Walter turned out to be a wonderful kisser. Instead of not wanting to be touched, I longed for his arms around me and loved to place my hand in his. It was a new type of passion for me, and I craved pressing myself up against him to breathe in his woody aftershave and feel his smooth, shaven face against my own. Around Walter I felt happy, warm, and excited, regardless of the little voice inside me reminding me to be realistic. I knew deep down I could never marry a Catholic, and I could never bear to have my children raised Catholic, as Walter would undoubtedly insist. Those thoughts brought severe pain, so I worked tremendously hard to push images of our inevitable breakup out of my mind. I was falling more and more in love with him with each passing day. I ached to be with Walter and felt hot energy course through me every time I saw his face. The way he looked at me was so powerful. He didn't have to say anything or do anything because just the way he looked at me told me, showed me, proved to me that he loved me. No human had ever loved me the way that my Walter loved me. How could I ever bear the excruciating agony of having to give him up?

We had dated for a year when Walter said he wanted to take me up to Maine. The girls at the shop were almost more excited than I was about the extended trip. I knew that it would be a wonderful time of sightseeing and relaxing at places I had never been to before. My trust in Walter was complete, and once again, he didn't disappoint me since he was the perfect gentleman. He even booked us two separate rooms although it cost him a great deal more money. The best part of our vacation was that he continued treating me like I was really something special even when there was no one else we knew around to see it. This made his love for me all the more real, and with this new tangibility, I began to think that maybe my prince, like Cinderella's, had finally come to rescue me after all. Perhaps, I could actually have a happy ending?

Chapter 20

MARRIAGE, REJECTION, AND EXCOMMUNICATION

It took me three long years, but after excessive inner turmoil, fervent prayer, and multiple conversations with wise people whom I trusted, I finally accepted and acknowledged that I was never going to find a Lutheran who loved me the way that Walter Belinsky loved me. Besides, was I really willing to give up all that I loved about Walter in order to marry a Lutheran man whom I didn't love? The answer suddenly became as clear as just cleaned, spotless windows. I didn't like to say it out loud, but I loved Walter. My three years with him and my continual reading of my Bible gave me the wisdom to see that what was really important about Walter's religious faith was that he was a follower of Jesus Christ. Catholic, Lutheran, Baptist, Methodist, Presbyterian—weren't we all just followers of Jesus Christ? Weren't we all equally sinners infinitely thankful for grace? Wasn't believing in the birth, crucifixion, and resurrection of Jesus the most important thing to us all? It was our own human failings that caused us to split up our denominations and churches in a way that God never intended. Humans separated themselves based on personal likes and dislikes of various practices, formats, and traditions, which is not God's fault. I decided that I could give up on being the wife of a Lutheran, but I would not give up on being a Lutheran myself and bringing my children up as such. If you recognize this as selfishness, you are correct in your observation. I was selfish. If you think that I was testing Walter to prove to myself how much he loved me, you may be right once again.

Then I learned from Edna Edelmann that Walter's parents were completely against us marrying because I was a Lutheran. Joe Belinsky told me that their mother was continuously torturing Walter with her anti-Wanda nagging, scolding, and threatening. I told Walter to stay away from me for three months so that I could see how much I missed him. I figured he would also get an enjoyable reprieve from his mother. His response was, "I know what I want, and I'm not going to stay away!" I saw that regardless, and in spite of the trying circumstances, Walter still loved me in a powerful way. I knew that he would fight to the end for me and just keep asking me to marry him until I gave him a positive answer and was definitive in my desire to be with him forever. When I finally came to see and understand all of these truths, and I just couldn't stand to make Walter suffer any more, I wholeheartedly agreed to marry him. Although, I made it extremely clear that I would be married in a Lutheran church and that I would remain a Lutheran. I even went so far as to tell him that our children would also be raised within the Lutheran Church. It was not a common thing in the 1940s for a woman to make any kind of demands on a man or to actually plan out her own future. That didn't stop me from telling Walter how it was going to be if he wanted to marry me. I was prepared for a battle and expecting one, but it never transpired because Walter immediately agreed and accepted my conditions. He understood who I was and what was important to me, and he loved me enough to make such a tremendous sacrifice. I knew that I had made the right decision, and I was elated about going ahead and marrying myself a Polish Catholic and becoming Wanda K. Belinsky.

In 1941, Walter Bernard Belinsky and I got married at St. Matthew's Lutheran Church. Walter looked breathtakingly handsome in his freshly pressed, new suit with a single, white rose on the lapel. His gray eyes sparkled with unbridled joy when he first saw me in my lovely, white satin wedding dress that cinched tightly around my waist and full bosom. I usually hated to see my face in photographs and even sometimes scratched out my countenance leaving only my body, but our wedding picture was different. I recognized that I looked beautiful with my ebony hair perfectly styled against the alabaster skin of my face. My dark eyes and lips sang out my joy in celebrating the moment. That treasured wedding day photograph would hang on the wall across from my bed for the rest of my life.

Everyone on my side of the family attended our nuptials, but Walter's irate parents refused to come following through on their threats to turn their backs on him if he married me. It seemed uniquely ironic that my father, who I felt had rejected me in my childhood, actually and literally stood up for me at my wedding. He not only attended, but he even walked me down the aisle and into the hands of Walter, despite the fact that I was not marrying a Lutheran as I'm sure he had intended. In fact, I was actually marrying a Catholic! Catholicism was supposed to be my religious foe. Wasn't it blasphemy when Walter prayed to the Virgin Mary? He owned prayer beads and a crucifix, which made him a devout Catholic, right? I waited for my father to remind me that Catholics were the ones who confessed their sins to a priest instead of directly to Christ Jesus and who dared to think Hail Marys instead of grace would save them. Didn't that just burn my father up? Before the wedding, I worried that he would abandon me again or stand up in front of everyone at the church and denounce me once more as Schlechta Wanda, but he didn't.

If my father was angry or disappointed, he didn't let on to me, and his feelings about my marriage remained a mystery. As I've said earlier, the thing that truly mattered to me was that Walter was a Christian, meaning that he believed that Jesus Christ alone had saved him. Did Father feel the same way? I tried not to let past paternal bitterness and hurt seep into my mind, but I secretly wondered if my father was only here at my wedding to ensure that I never came back to the farm. Or was it possible that Father was sincerely happy for me? Could he actually be proud? Whatever my father thought or felt, I cannot say because, as always, he never discussed it with me and never lost his stern expression, even in my wedding pictures. I told myself that what was important and mattered most was that my father was at my marriage ceremony and its celebration. That day, my father's actions spoke louder than his words ever could.

Even in Walter's tremendous joy at us becoming man and wife, I knew that he mourned the devastating blow of his parents' complete rejection and desertion on our wedding day and afterwards. I couldn't comprehend how they could be so cruel after all that Walter had done for them, including paying for their house and otherwise financially supporting them. He had been a loyal and obedient son in every way except that his heart loved who it loved—me. In every other aspect, except my religion, I was acceptable and desirable to my Belinsky in-laws, but me being a Lutheran and remaining a Lutheran was a non-negotiable deal breaker for them. They wounded Walter deeply, and for that I was fiercely angry with his parents. Only out of respect for Walter and to heed his wishes did I go against my own rampant desire to verbally confront them and stayed quiet. Even though Walter tried to cover up his oozing hurt, in the still moments I would catch him staring sadly into space and knew that he was aching for his parents to speak to him and to allow him to visit.

Walter's heart was further broken and irreparably injured when the Catholic Church kicked him out. He was absolutely destroyed when he received a formal letter stating that he had been permanently excommunicated from the Catholic Church for marrying a Lutheran. Walter was further admonished and humiliated when he was physically barred from entering the church that he had diligently attended his entire life. Just like me, church and faith were an essential part of who Walter was as a human being. When his beloved Catholic Church expelled him, he was forever after crushed to his core and wearily bore the painful injuries inflicted on him by their earthly rejection. If Catholicism had been an actual person, I would have had a terribly difficult time keeping myself from punching it right in the face and spitting on it as I walked away. Thank the good Lord, Walter was much calmer and more reasonable than I. He didn't blame God for the human failings of the people who represented the Catholic Church. He felt only deep sadness; whereas, I felt fierce anger.

Chapter 21
MY BASEMENT BEAUTY SHOP AND MY BABIES

Walter had saved up quite a bit of money before we met, so as soon as we were engaged, he had our first and only house built at 9619 Leon Street in Philadelphia. I couldn't wait to move in as soon as we were married. Not only was it our very own, but I could finally get rid of my old address. I would never have to live at 6114 Alma Street, Philadelphia, Pennsylvania, ever again. Yes, I did say "Alma" Street, as in the dreaded name of my stepmother, and no, I never found it amusing that out of all the hundreds of names of roads in Philly, I would have ended up living on the one with her name.

The new house on a corner property off of Leon Street sat up on a hill and was red brick with white shutters that had the image of a sailboat carved into each one. Our home was two stories plus a full finished basement that included windows, and we even had a two-car garage. There was one large full bath upstairs and a half bath downstairs. I served all of our meals in our formal dining room using the beautiful, cherry-colored wood dining room furniture that Walter bought me right after we were married. The downstairs also had a small kitchen and a living room with a lovely fireplace. Throughout the house, we had gorgeous, light-colored wood floors that I covered with fancy rugs, as well as tile in the bathrooms and linoleum in the kitchen. Just like back on the farm, I scrubbed those wood floors on my hands and knees with a soft brush and white cloths. The only difference was that now I waited a few days between cleanings instead of doing them twice a day. People don't really know dirt and sweat unless they know the kind that comes from farming. Since I no longer lived on a farm but in a neighborhood with grass and sidewalks, I didn't have to contend with the burdensome and overwhelming anxiety of watching things I'd just finished making perfectly clean and orderly immediately become saturated with grime, soil, and dust.

My favorite part of our whole place was the front porch overlooking the lush, green lawn and the two goliath oak trees that framed our front yard. I planted shrubs and flowers all around the entire house, and I particularly enjoyed sitting outside on the front porch to absorb nature through my five senses. The cool evening breezes brought the scents of roses and jasmine as I enjoyed counting the infinite number of glowing, yellow lightning bugs that scurried furtively above the lawn at dusk. Sitting there, I could relax and reflect when alone or, better yet, talk incessantly with anyone who decided to join me. We lived on a corner lot, and I treasured our good-sized front and back yards, which were hard to come by in the city. Directly across the street from our house was a golf course with green rolling hills, large patches of trees, and a wide creek that could only be crossed via a small, curved footbridge. It was a blessing that the wonderful location of our home made it easy to imagine myself as being out in the open countryside instead of in the heart of the bustling City of Brotherly Love. I turned our backyard into a nature haven. I placed my garden in the farthest end of the terrace and loaded it full of beans, carrots, onions, tomatoes, lettuce, corn, cauliflower, and broccoli. My rose garden flourished on the side of the yard that bordered the sidewalk. Using some of Mother's rose bushes from the farm and others from local nurseries, I slowly expanded my treasure until I had the most colorful and fragrant roses in the entire neighborhood. It warmed my heart to see people stop and admire them. Breathing in the roses' potent fragrances, many a passerby would smile and step back to fully take in the rainbow assortment of different colored wonders.

Since I had always enjoyed hearing and seeing birds, I set up numerous bird houses and feeders and even a large, white bird bath. In between hanging up wet clothes on the clotheslines and doing other chores, I sometimes found a moment to just sit in a yard chair and watch the lively birds. My favorites were the bright red cardinals, but I also enjoyed pudgy bluebirds, yellow finches, tiny wrens, and even noisy hummingbirds in the summer. How thankful I was to be able to sit and rest for a few minutes without being cussed at or berated. To have the hot sun warming my face and to feel the gentle wind blowing wisps of my hair was pure enchantment. I felt that getting to listen to the animated conversations of birds singing into the quiet of my afternoons was truly more than I deserved.

The second floor of our house had three bedrooms, one of which had a door that opened up to a flat roof to be used for sunning. Another of the bedrooms had stairs built into the closet allowing me to walk up into the spacious attic where I stored numerous items. Little did I know that one day my children would enjoy pretending that the hidden attic stairs were magical and would often climb them in order to be transported into a secret world of glorious adventures. Our one full bathroom was large and situated across the hall from our oversized master bedroom. I considered the bathroom to be quite fancy because it had a separate shower placed beside the sunken bathtub. I sewed delicate, flowery curtains to cover the large window that faced the backyard and designed the entire space to look clean and lovely. There were many times that I couldn't stifle my laughter while sitting on the porcelain toilet comparing my present fancy bathroom to the bare outhouse that I had used as a child. There were no more smelly chamber pots under the bed for this girl and no more dreaded, long walks to the cold outhouse in the middle of the night.

"What are you giggling about in there?" Walter called out to me one evening as I sat on the commode.

"It's just that my bum is very happy," I yelled back before bursting into even louder, sustained laughter.

Walter insisted that his wife was never going to have to work as hard as his mother. Mrs. Belinsky had been forced to work long, demanding hours outside of the home in order to rescue her family from the threatening power of financial ruin. Memories of her hardships overpowered Walter's brain making him adamant about not wanting me to work outside of our home at all. I decided that I could honor Walter's wishes by being a housewife and still make myself happy by doing people's hair in my basement. Soon there were numerous friends, clients, and family members who came to me to get their hair done. I had a comfortable chair for them to sit in and a large salon-type dresser with multiple drawers and a three-tiered mirror. My capes, clips, scissors, curlers, brushes, combs, and more all fit nicely within or on top of that beloved dresser. I had all the supplies that I needed including a special sink to wash hair and a heated dryer to fit down over people's heads. Sometimes I didn't charge anything unless they really insisted because Walter was such a good provider that I really didn't need any money, although it still felt empowering to be earning some. I had always had a talent for fixing hair, and now I could use my gift and my education to provide a service for people simply because I enjoyed it. Hearing clients say, "No one can cut hair like Wanda!" nourished me, and my dessert was all of the people, especially my family members, who faithfully returned week after week. I particularly remember my sister-in-law Agnes and my sisters Paula and Martha coming to my basement beauty shop every time they needed a perm. Those were always special family times because they were filled with lots of juicy gossip and hours of uncontrollable laughter. Gone were my worries about survival. The vivid nightmares of my childhood fled. Vanquished were my piercing night visions of a pitiful, damaged teenager left alone and virtually penniless by her father on a dirty, crumbling street in downtown Philadelphia. My daily joy now was just in living and in being free to make the people around me happy like I was.

It wasn't long before I became pregnant. Even in my ninth month, I remained thin with only the slightest baby bump. Most people didn't suspect our exciting news and were surprised when we told them about a Belinsky baby. I wanted to name the baby Linda if it was a girl, but my brother Albert's wife, Susanne, had her daughter first and named her Linda, so I decided on the name Judy. Walter and I had our beautiful, blonde-haired Judy in 1943. She was a relaxed baby who rarely cried. She was very easy to care for, and I adjusted quickly to being a mother, even foolishly letting myself believe that this mothering thing wasn't nearly as tough as people said.

My doctor and everybody else told me that I could not get pregnant again while I was nursing Judy. That was a complete load of crap because I got pregnant again just about two months after Judy was born. Dierdre was born in 1944 making our girls less than a year apart. When Dee-Dee arrived, I took Judy off of the bottle but found that she was constantly grabbing Dee's bottle and drinking it herself. This would send Dee into ear piercing crying fits, and I couldn't turn my back for a minute without it happening. In desperation, I figured out that I could take a Coke bottle, put a nipple on it, and fill it with milk for Judy before she went to bed. This seemed to help cut down on the baby bottle thievery. Judy loved it so much that she refused to give up the practice until she was four years old. People assumed that the girls were twins throughout their childhood since they were the same petite size and looked so much alike with their blonde curls. I liked to sew adorable, matching outfits for them and did for as long as they would let me.

Dee-Dee loved to hear me tell the story of how I came up with her name. My being so loquacious made the anecdote all the more entertaining for her. The gist of it was this. Most afternoons, I would faithfully listen to my favorite soap opera on the radio while I ironed our clothes. It kept me entertained as I went through the monotony of creating perfect creases and destroying all wrinkles. One of the best loved characters in the soap opera was named Dierdre, and they called her Dee-Dee for short. She was packed with personality and wasn't afraid to speak her mind. She frequently used her intelligence and wit to get the best of the men who chased after her. Even though I could only hear her voice and had to imagine what the character of Dee-Dee looked like, I could tell that she was animated and dramatic. Life just oozed from her, and I loved that! I decided that if our second baby ended up being a girl, I wanted to name her Dierdre Ann Belinsky and would call her Dee-Dee for short.

Dee-Dee lived up to her name; she was brimming over with energy and personality from the start. That proved a good thing because it always seemed to me that she was trying hard to keep up with her older, much admired sister. I can still picture

Dee-Dee's little legs frantically pedaling round and round on her tricycle in an attempt to keep up with athletic Judy, who continually sped ahead on her two-wheeled bike leaving Dee-Dee far behind. When they were a bit older, Dee-Dee's not wanting to be left out seemed to turn into a need to constantly compete with Judy. Judy was always laid back and carefree; whereas, Dee-Dee was more high-strung and always harshly pushed herself. Her feisty temperament and strong-willed disposition matched mine, which wasn't always a good combination. We were too much alike to always get along, and I undoubtedly got on her nerves more so than I did Judy's. I didn't think that I was pretty while I was growing up, and Dee-Dee seemed to inherit that insecurity from me as well. The irony was that for several years people continued to ask me if Judy and Dee-Dee were twins, so how Dee-Dee could think that her sister was beautiful and yet not see it in herself was puzzling.

I made sure that both girls took piano lessons when they were young. Judy went on to play the string bass while Dee-Dee chose the cello. Judy enjoyed sports and excelled at volleyball in high school. She first wanted to be a nurse, so she worked as a candy striper at Hannamen Hospital in Philadelphia. Judy's high school counselor suggested that she try something new in college, so Judy decided to be a teacher. At an early age, Dee-Dee learned that her best place to shine was in academics. She was extremely bright but still studied constantly, so it was no wonder that she always achieved straight A's. Dee-Dee grew to become Dee and was an officer of the Future Teachers of America club, president of her church youth group, and an honor roll student. She was also the valedictorian of her class. Dee clearly wanted to excel in academics, so I didn't have to compel her at all. Her goal, starting in elementary school, was to study hard in order to get scholarship money for college, and she succeeded. Dee had always wanted to be a teacher, and she pursued it wholeheartedly in college, following her sister to Concordia College in Bronxville, New York, and then Concordia College in River Forest, Illinois. I was very gratified that both of my girls graduated from college with Dee going on to graduate school to obtain her master's in teaching language arts. There was never any doubt in my mind that my daughters would get all of the education that they wanted and deserved and would be able to pursue the career paths that they chose. I was so proud when they did.

Walter loved both of his daughters very much and was extremely proud of them too. He always wanted the girls to look and feel well dressed. I was an excellent seamstress and often made my dress suits and matching outfits for them, but Walter still insisted that we go downtown to the big department stores like John Wanamaker or Strawbridge and Clothier to buy many of our dress clothes. The girls and I secretly loved these excursions even though I always put up a fuss. Walter also liked to buy me fancy hats while we were in downtown Philly, and I am so thankful now that he did. I acquired quite the colorful hat collection over the years and kept them safely stored in ornate boxes and stuffed with tissue paper until I was ready to wear them. It was something special and exciting for me every time I was able to look at my hats and to turn them over gently in my hands. I can still see each of them vividly in my mind: one was covered with feathers dyed dark blue, another shiny black, and (one of my favorites) a flaming red feather headpiece that I had to pin to my hair. Other hats were made of velvet, satin, and cool silk. Some were lacy, while others had bold colored bows and ribbons or were more subdued in hues of tan and brown. There were hats with wide brims and hats without brims at all in every imaginable color. Walter thought that I looked beautiful in every single one of those hats and told me so often that I even started to believe him. It's funny how sometimes the smallest things, like hats, can make such an impression on a person's life that they live on forever in memory and are able to stir up happy emotions even in dark times.

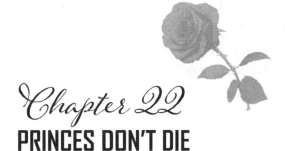

Chapter 22

PRINCES DON'T DIE

Since you now know some of the joys of my life with Walter, please allow me to also share some of the bitter pains that plagued me during our time together because that too is my story. Where to begin? As I shared earlier, Judy was an easy baby, and life continued on easily after I gave birth to her, until suddenly, it didn't. While I was pregnant with Dierdre, Walter developed a rough cough and began having night sweats and a high fever. I encouraged him to stay home from work and get some rest because in his fatigued state, he would never improve. He refused and quickly started losing weight. It had only taken Walter a few weeks of married life, with me cooking him hearty meals three times a day, to put on fifteen pounds. But now he was losing all of that healthy weight and becoming even thinner than before our wedding when he had literally lived off of hot dogs. One fateful, moonlit night, he shot up in the bed clutching his chest and coughing uncontrollably. Walter tried to cover his mouth but sputum covered in blood shot out of it and spewed across our yellow bedspread. "Walter! Walter!" I screamed. After chest X-rays and skin testing, the doctors told us that it was tuberculosis, a highly infectious and dreaded, deadly disease that was easily transmitted from person to person. They prescribed extended treatments with two anti-TB drugs that would mean months in a facility. When harshly questioned, the doctors also admitted that the drugs could be administered at home. After much prayer and conversation, Walter and I decided that I would care for him at our house.

My years of being a clean freak would serve me well as I endeavored to care for Walter while protecting Judy and myself from the same fate. But Walter was still withering away before my very eyes. I knew that not being able to go to work and make more money for us was killing him. He apologized profusely for everything that I was having to do, and I wiped tears from his pale face while he mumbled about how he never wanted his wife to have to work so hard. He reminded me that he had sworn his wife would never be forced to work long hours outside of the home like his own mother had. Walter fretted that if he died, I would eventually have to find full-time employment in order to provide for our children. He couldn't stand the prospect of me having to earn money once his savings ran out.

"I want to provide for you Wanda and to give you everything you deserve! I am so sorry, so very sorry!" he wailed. I wiped my fingertips across his furrowed brow.

"Walter, it is not your fault. Everything will be okay. The Lord will provide," I whispered soothingly. He clutched my hand in his and held it tightly to his chest as he began to pray aloud begging God not to let him die. I closed my eyes and tilted my face up towards the ceiling uttering inaudible, concurring words towards heaven.

I barely made it out of the room before tears gushed from my eyes. Hurrying towards the basement, I made sure to close the heavy wooden door behind me before scrambling down the steps. I didn't want Walter or anybody else to hear me crying. Backing up to the one wall without any windows, I slid down it until I sat on the cold floor with my knees tight to my chest, which was quite a feat considering I was very pregnant. I howled like some kind of mortally wounded creature and banged the palms of both of my hands against the wall behind me. "Oh God! Please, please help me! I don't want my children to lose their father before they even get to know him!"

I sat there for a long time sobbing until I could calm myself. It was then with a shiver that I remembered one of my most vivid, reoccurring childhood dreams. I had dreamed that my vitriolic father was dead because his liver was destroyed by drinking. In those old, nocturnal images, I would see myself standing by his grave not shedding a tear. This dream typically manifested itself after Father had beaten me within an inch of my life all the while screaming "Schlechta Wanda, Schlechta Wanda!" In the morning, I always felt overwhelming guilt that my dreams were manifesting themselves in such a way as to easily convict me in a court of law if the jury were trying to determine whether or not I wanted my father dead. Now, here I was years later hoping, praying, begging God for a completely opposite thing from what I thought I wanted as a child. This time, I wanted to keep the father in my life alive. This time, I wanted my own children to have a father who lived.

Chapter 23

WHAT AM I GOING TO DO WITH THIS ONE?

A week later, I awoke at 3:00 a.m. to the pain and pressure of contractions. I quickly got up, showered, dressed, put on makeup, and fixed my hair. As planned, I called Martha to tell her that I was in labor and needed Paula and her to come over and take care of Walter and Judy. I then calmly phoned my across-the-street neighbor, Margaret, to let her know that the time had arrived for her to take me to the hospital. I carried my bags to the side door and looked around to make sure I had everything ready for my sisters to use while they cared for my husband and baby girl. After going back upstairs and whispering sweet words of love over Judy, I blew her kisses through the air not wanting to awaken her with my touch. I then leaned over Walter and woke him up to let him know that our baby was coming. He looked at me with such love in his eyes and hugged me close before kissing the top of my head.

"I love you," he said.

"I know you do. Thank you for loving me," I answered. I kissed the top of his hand, and he smiled in acknowledgment because he knew that I was telling him without using words that I loved him too.

I sat in the plain hospital room alone, except for the doctor and nurses, and contemplated with fearful anticipation the arrival of my second child. This time my water broke quickly, and the painful contractions were frequent and violent. Then, in a blur, she was there. I heard crying and crisp, raised voices. Someone was saying, "It's a girl!" My body and my mind were heavy and exhausted, just wanting to sleep. I spotted a tiny infant, my daughter, before I turned my weary head and closed my eyes. The nurses seemed alarmed that I didn't want to hold or feed my child. They prodded me to try.

"Don't you want to see your beautiful baby?"

They became noticeably anxious when I said, "Not really."

An older, gray-haired nurse turned her frowning face towards me and grunted, "What? Did your husband die in the war or something?"

"My husband didn't have to go fight when the war started due to his older age," I mumbled. "And he won't have to go now because he's sick," I added.

"Well, then you are one of the lucky ones girlie," she said briskly while raising one of her eyebrows and scowling at me.

"Oh yes! I sure am lucky," I replied in the most sarcastic tone I could muster. I could feel the blood rushing to my face. "I have a husband dying from TB and an eleven-month-old at home. Now, you tell me! What am I going to do with this one?" I gestured towards the tiny, squirming bundle in the other nurse's arms. How could I be saying such things? But I felt so depressed at that moment that somehow I didn't care. "Please give me a few moments to rest and pull myself together," I managed to utter while trying to hide the umbrage in my voice. They hesitated but then took Dierdre from the room. "God please help me. Please help me do this," I said aloud.

After laying there in silence for a very long while, I slowly felt a feeling of warmth pass over my body. It reminded me of laying with Walter on the summer sand at the Shore and feeling my whole body tingle as the hot sun warmed my skin. That was such a delightful and relaxing sensation. I thought about how fortunate I had been to be able to enjoy such moments every time Walter took me to Wildwood, New Jersey. I also grasped that the warm sensation I reveled in now was of a different kind. It was the acknowledgment that the unique child who had kicked me and bounced around inside of me for nine months was now out in the world. Who and what would she be? Would she look like me or like her father? All at once, I felt overwhelmingly thankful for my many blessings. A nurse timidly peeked inside my hospital door, and I raised my voice to call out to her, "I'm ready to be with my baby now," and miraculously, I was.

I looked down at the tiny baby in my arms. Huge absorbing eyes stared unblinking up at me. She looked more like a perfect baby doll then a human child. Tremendous dark eyes and a perfectly round face rested gently in the crook of my arm. I recognized her father's pudgy cheeks and smiled. I went to touch some of her downy soft dark eyelashes, and she grabbed my finger with an unrelenting grip. "My, you are strong Dee-Dee! You are tough and determined just like your mother," I said, and knew it to be true. I felt that my Dee-Dee had many gifts all packed into one tiny, blonde-haired little infant. She was such a minuscule thing, but I knew that she would do great good in the world. I would soon come to recognize my own Konschak feistiness in her determined, strong nature as well as her father's organizational skills, efficiency, and intelligence in her daily life. Dee-Dee proved throughout the years that she was definitely a true combination of us both.

After a few days in the hospital, Dee-Dee and I eagerly went home. I thanked Martha and Paula profusely for caring for Judy and Walter while I was away. I loved my sisters so much. I wondered how I ever could have done this thing called life without them. I was once again overwhelmed with thankfulness; this time, it was for all my siblings. Maybe we weren't still living all together on the farm, but we remained connected and intricate in each other's lives, which was a true blessing. As soon as my sisters pulled away from my house, I missed them, and a sense of aloneness slithered over me. I knew that they had their own lives to attend to, so I would never have dreamed of asking them to stay with me longer. Besides, Wanda could always handle anything and everything! My pride wouldn't allow my mind to even consider asking for additional help.

Chapter 24
OVERCOMING THE WORLD

I finished giving Walter a sponge bath, and he gratefully thanked me as I headed to the bathroom to empty his bedpan. I looked outside the window and noticed that it was not very bright. Turning around, I caught a glimpse of myself in the bathroom mirror and was startled by the grisly reflection that peered back at me. The bedpan tumbled from my hands and clamored angrily to the floor. It was no wonder that I had terrified myself. My dirty hair was matted down to my head. It had not been washed or even brushed for several days and lay limply over my sunken eyes. The dark circles underneath my eyes matched the color of my pupils. I resembled a hideous zombie and was actually shocked by my own thinness and pallor. It is terrifying to be virtually unrecognizable to oneself. I felt like a fake version of Wanda. I wished that the real me was somehow floating above the ground like a stunningly bright angel because the dreadfully unkempt person in the mirror couldn't possibly be me. Wanda Konschak Belinsky would never allow herself to look like that!

There was no time to wallow in self-pity or to be in a state of shock because at that moment twelve-month-old Judy woke up from her brief nap and began crying in her crib. Her wails woke up newly born Dee-Dee who commenced howling from her bassinet to let me know that I was late for her feeding. The sound of a sobbing infant was a tortuous noise that my high-strung nerves could never bear for long. To me, a baby howling was a far worse annoyance than any other kind of disconcerting racket, including the sound of fingernails on a chalkboard. I simply could not stand to hear a child cry; I had to immediately help the little one calm herself. Both of the girls crying and needing me at the same time was nothing new. But this time it was pushing me over the edge. I was mentally exhausted, completely sleep deprived, and horribly neglectful of my own physical needs. I smelled like sweat, baby vomit, and feces. I didn't know what day it was or whether it was dawn or dusk. "I'm losing it," I said to myself right before I heard the jingle jingle of a bell ringing. The sound came from across the hall and was signifying that my dying Walter needed my help. "I can't do this," I mumbled and just stood there.

Feeling dizzy, I plummeted down the stairs, through the dining room, into the kitchen, and out the back door. I barreled towards my rose bushes brushing aside cloth diapers that were long since dried on the clothesline. I pushed myself into the middle of several rows of rose bushes and collapsed down onto the cool dirt. My instinct was to find safety with my mother. The closest thing I had to her was my rainbow of rose bushes because I had transplanted many of them from the farm in Hartly to my own yard. I lay amongst her roses and stared up into the darkening sky weeping loudly. "God, I don't know how much more of this I can take," I sobbed. "This world is too much for me!" The sounds of silence loomed all around and buried themselves underneath my body as it lay motionless and helpless on the ground. It was odd because I usually heard the lovely sounds of birds chirping along with the clicking, buzzing racket of bugs whenever I was outside. The feeling of being empty but at the same time completely filled with a gnawing nothingness overpowered me. I thought that perhaps I would never again rise up from the rich, black soil. Instead of just having my body touching the earth, maybe my whole human shell would sink into the ground, and then my soul could be lifted up to heaven. "Dust to dust and ashes to ashes," I whispered to myself. It seemed to me to be a fitting end to my life in a merciless world that had always tried to beat me down.

I know that some people won't believe this, but I promise you that at that moment, I heard a voice. Whether it was audible to others or just inside my head, I can't tell you, but I very distinctly heard: "Fear not! For I have overcome the world!" The voice was powerful, yet kind, and I felt the strength of the words descend onto me like a warm blanket while at the same time my eager ears absorbed the soothing sounds. Instead of being anxious or scared, I felt peace and calm—two things that I hadn't felt in over a month. I knew with complete certainty that it was the peace that only God can give. I lay there for a long time and basked in the warm glow of the Son. Smiling to myself, I understood that the Lord had indeed provided for me like Mother always said He would. I knew that whatever happened, God was still for me. That voice was a reminder that no matter how difficult my life on Earth might be, God had already won the final battle because Jesus rose from the dead. That victory meant hope for this short life, and more importantly, for the next infinite one. I could not and would not let my current circumstances destroy me! Leaving all my angst behind, I mustered up the last tiny bit of determined feistiness from within me, got up off the damp ground, and walked back into the house renewed. As I did so, I breathed in the sweet aroma of glorious roses that floated all around me, and once again, I could hear the brave song of a brilliantly red cardinal that sat perched above me in my favorite sugar maple tree. "I can do this!" I shouted.

Chapter 25
DEATH HAS TO PRECEDE A RESURRECTION

Months passed and Walter was not improving. My church family along with my sisters and brothers all supported me with their visits, cards, and food deliveries. I coveted their assistance but at the same time was terrified to acknowledge what they foresaw as my doomed future. They all rallied around my Walter and me because they felt that it would not be long before he died. "You know Walter never gives up when it comes to you, Wanda," my older sister Jule said to me one Sunday afternoon after church. It was then that I recognized that she and I were probably the only ones still holding out hope for Walter to have a miraculous recovery.

One Friday evening after hours of fitful blood-filled coughing, Walter couldn't even lift his defeated head from the pillow. I kissed him on the forehead and walked downstairs to our telephone in the kitchen so that he couldn't hear me. I opened up my blue leather address book to where I had written Walter's parents' home telephone number in the B section. Walter had tried to speak to them numerous times in the years since our wedding but had been unsuccessful. I had never called their number before, but that day I did so with determination. After three dreadfully long rings, someone picked up the receiver, and I heard a woman's voice.

"This is Mary Belinsky, may I help you?"

"This is Wanda, and if you and John ever want to see your son alive again in this life, you had better get over here because he is dying," I said sternly and hung up. I knew that it was rude to hang up on her and impolite to call at that time of night, but I didn't care. They knew that Walter was sick and hadn't once checked up on him. As far as I was concerned, she was lucky to have eluded a nasty cussing from her Jezebel-like daughter-in-law. Mary and John knew where we lived. I had seen them drive by our house a couple times during its construction and many times after its completion, but they never stopped and spoke with us. They had never even met their own grandchildren. I honestly don't know if it was kindness or bitterness that made me call Walter's parents that day, but I was absolutely certain that I had to tell them that Walter was going to die.

I was experiencing a clash of incompatible feelings because even though I was irate at the Belinskys for forsaking their son, I also felt sorry for them. Here they were about to lose another one of their children. Walter's youngest brother had died in childhood, and his only sister, dear Irene, had died from tuberculosis (TB) even before we were married. It had only been a year since Walt's brother, Frank, had also died from TB. I couldn't imagine losing four of my children while I still walked the Earth. My pity shifted to anger, though, the more I thought about the pain they had inflicted on their son, my husband. "They will be sorry that they wasted precious time with him when he is gone," I thought to myself as I splashed water from the kitchen sink onto my face to disguise the path of my tears.

And then it happened. The time of letting go finally came. It was time to say "goodbye" to anger, disappointment, grief, bitterness, and arrogance, and the Belinskys did just that. Early the next morning, there was a slight knock on the door, and I went quickly to open it. I held Dee-Dee on my hip, and Judy was tightly gripping my long apron in order to procure my attention. I couldn't speak. Before me stood Walter's uneasy parents. Their hungry eyes darted to their beautiful, blonde granddaughters before settling on my face.

"We are so sorry," Mrs. Belinsky uttered passionately.

"Please accept our heartfelt apology," added Mr. Belinsky.

"Come in." I invited them inside with a gesture of my free hand. "You need to see Walter. Please follow me." I situated the girls in their large, wooden playpen loaded with toys and led my in-laws upstairs. They followed with hesitation, no doubt overcome with guilt as I ushered them into the room of their dying, prodigal son now finally returning home.

All of my life I had heard people talk about how "the Lord works in mysterious ways" and how "God can bring some good out of the most terrible situations." After almost losing Walter, I could recognize the truth of these adages in my own life. If Walter hadn't gotten so gravely ill and been to the point of death, his parents would have never been convicted in their hearts to reunite with him. It was his imminent death that spurred them to the action of reconciliation. Once Walter's parents could again show their love for him, they were able to obtain the additional treasure of getting to know and love their granddaughters. Perhaps the beautiful life embodied in Judy and Dee-Dee showed them that God's plans could not be thwarted, even if they weren't the plans that Mary and John would have chosen themselves. They could finally see me as their daughter-in-law, Wanda Konschak Belinsky, instead of only as that bad, Lutheran girl who had stolen their beloved son.

Miraculously, within weeks of reuniting with his parents, Walter began to show steady signs of improvement. He no longer coughed up blood and was putting on weight. He started getting out of bed more and more and even began preparing to return to work. The doctors said that it must have been that last round of antibiotics that ultimately saved him. But I knew better than that. I knew that it was God who had ordained Walter's resurrection because Walter's time on Earth wasn't complete. It was God who decided that my husband wouldn't yet leave and would even live to enjoy all seven of his grandchildren. I was filled with gratitude that Walter wasn't taken away from me like my mother had been. When Walter was first diagnosed with tuberculosis, the fear of once again having to parent and run a household by myself had kept me awake many nights. As a fifteen-year-old, it had been the farm that I needed to oversee and Albert and Martha who I needed to nurture once our dear Mother had died. The whole nightmarish scenario seemed to be happening again when Walter's death appeared sure. Except this time, it would be my home in Philadelphia and the lives of Judy and Dee-Dee that I would be solely responsible for sustaining. When I recognized that my fearfulness had been a lie because Walter was going to live, I was overcome with joy. I shut that lie up really quickly and refused to listen to it any longer. Awe and amazement just spilled out of me once I could see how God had used the powerful love of Walter's parents to heal the part of his heart that was needed to cure his tuberculosis-ridden lungs.

Chapter 26
KEEPING THE CATHOLIC OUT

Even though Walter's parents accepted him back, the Catholic Church did not. It actually wasn't until after Walter died at the age of eighty-one that they sent me a formal letter stating that they had retracted Walter's excommunication and had accepted him back into the Catholic fold. That really burned me up and filled me with an anger that was all too familiar. The expression "too little too late" took on a whole new meaning, and I am not proud of what I thought or what I said as Judy, Dee, and I sat around the dining room table reading aloud the plethora of condolence cards.

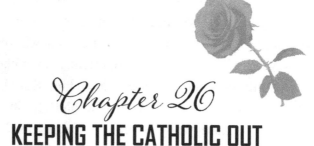

I was forced to think back over the many years in which Walter never could bring himself to attend the Lutheran church with our daughters and me except on rare, special occasions. Every Sunday after we left for Sunday school and church, he settled himself down into his favorite green and white striped chair and fervently read his Bible and the monthly devotionals that I brought home for him. He had kept his relationship with Christ, which was the most important thing, but it was terrible and tragic to me and to our daughters that he was unable to bring himself to again regularly cross the threshold of a church for a worship service. What fellowship and love he could have experienced with us if only he had returned to a church community! I knew that the church could have once again provided a second family to him just as it had in his childhood, but he wouldn't allow it. He was never again a regular part of a community of worship after his excommunication, and it seared my heart. The Catholic Church was wrong to excommunicate him, and my Walter was also wrong in that he allowed that biting hurt to be a lifelong excuse. My girls and I forever longed to have him with us like the other husbands and fathers who weekly attended church with their families. Both Judy and Dee took the biblical principle of being *equally yoked* very seriously when it came time for them to date and to search for a future husband. It was no surprise to me that they were both determined to have a husband who would go to church with his family every Sunday. They wanted their own children to have the blessing of attending church with both a mother and a father, which was something that they had never had.

I personally have always felt like the most loving thing that I could do for my own children was to expose them to the grace of Jesus Christ. I fervently wanted them to have a powerful Christian upbringing to sustain them in the trials of this life and to bring them to the next one. But everything that I did at church, I did without the presence of their father. I often felt a sharp pain in my chest as I viewed the other husbands attending church with their families. It greatly saddened me that my girls could not share such a powerful part of their lives with their father. I saw that they were sometimes confused and hurt by his absence. As they got older, they thankfully came to understand that Walter was a believer in Jesus Christ even though he didn't go to church. Judy and Dee may have accepted that their father chose to worship God at home, but they sure didn't like it one bit.

It was extremely upsetting for me to think about how much more precious time we all would have had together, if only he had joined us on Sundays. It could have been a soothing balm during the many years when he had to spend countless hours running his steel business in Trenton, New Jersey. We craved Walter's time and attention, which were quickly swallowed up by his job, and missed him terribly.

I took the girls to Redeemer Lutheran Church from birth until they left for college, and we three were happily and thoroughly a part of just about every aspect of that church. Judy and Dee were baptized and confirmed there, and we diligently attended Sunday school and other weekly activities. Both girls also attended Redeemer Lutheran Day School until they started ninth grade. I busied myself by working with Redeemer's Parent Association of Lutheran Schools and with the Lutheran Church Association on their hospitality and property committees. As an elected officer of the Ladies Guild (president and later other offices), I worked on numerous projects that enabled me to serve many people and to experience the palpable joy of selfless acts that my mother had talked about all those years before. Walter was correct when he said that I was always cooking or baking something delicious for a dinner or some other special event at church. We Lutherans loved our potlucks; that was for sure! I also served on the altar committee, helped teach Sunday school as Ms. Perrin's assistant, went to Bible study, organized church bazaars, and sewed quilts for the sickly. I made robes for the third through eighth grade children's choirs, acted as choir mother, prepared food to be given to the poor and the elderly, and in all other ways was a highly involved member of my church for sixty years. Phew! But I loved it! I really loved my church family, and they, in turn, loved me.

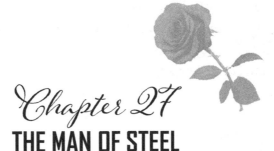

Chapter 27
THE MAN OF STEEL

Walter worked very hard for his boss at Precision Drawn Steel Company and had a high position, but he still had a dream to start his own steel cutting business. Before he could do that, he needed to put himself through business school. Walter knew he had to work full time during the day to provide money for us, so he decided to take night classes. My diligent and determined Walter somehow found the energy to work, attend classes, and study all within a twenty-four-hour day. I was so proud of him when he obtained his degree and so excited for him to move forward with the next part of his plan of becoming a successful business owner. Walter sought out a business partner and found one by the name of A. Farell who also worked at Precision Steel. Together they started Bel-Far Steel Company soon after Walter recovered from TB. I guessed that since Walter assumed more of the cost and the risk, our last name got to go first. I liked the company name. To me, it implied that *Belinsky* would *go far*, and I prayed that this new venture would. Bel-Far produced cold finished bars of steel by cutting down much larger pieces. They also cut steel into wire that could be made into coils or straight lengths and used to produce hangers. Their business cards and paper pads said that the steel wire they cut could be purchased in bright basic, black annealed, galvanized basic, or music spring. I didn't know what any of that meant, but I acted like I did. The company also sized steel to be used in drill rods and tools. My very thorough and organized Walter kept on top of everything needed to make Bel-Far a success, and its client list grew rapidly.

The partnership only lasted a few years before Walter bought Farell's part of the company. Walt simply told me that Farell had done something "inappropriate business-wise," and Walter felt he had no choice but to buy him out. I wanted to know details, but that is all he would tell me because my husband was not one to stir the pot, and he avoided gossip. Maybe Walter was afraid of what I might say or do to Farell if I knew all the details. That was most likely a smart decision on Walter's part. I guessed that maybe Farell took company money and Walter caught him. If that was the case, I think Walter was lenient in letting him off without pressing charges and merciful in paying him for his part in their joint enterprise. Walter decided to keep the original Bel-Far name even when he was the only owner because all the vendors knew him by that name, and it would make things easier and much less confusing for all parties involved.

Walter was very proud of the quality of his work and spent innumerable hours at his business and in his commute from Philadelphia to Trenton, New Jersey. He left before sunrise and returned home well after dark. People respected his effort and his honesty. Walt worked incredibly hard and after twenty-five years was faced with a dilemma. He began to ponder retirement within the next few years and started evaluating potential candidates who he deemed moral, honest, and hard-working enough to take over his company. The few worthy possibilities were not interested in undertaking such an endeavor or were already settled into a different career path. At the same time, the steel market was undergoing severe changes. Walter had always bought American steel and didn't want to have to buy the steel he used in his facility from a foreign country. When it became clear that he would have to go against his patriotic principals if he continued in the business, he decided to sell out rather than be forced to deal with steel that wasn't American made. Walter liquidated his entire business and retired, after which he never went back to New Jersey, not even once.

For the many years that Walter did have the business, I kept myself busy with trying to make Walter's brief time at home as wonderful as possible. He raved over my delicious cooking and couldn't get enough of my homemade pickles and olives. Walter liked things to be tidy and organized, and lucky for him, I was overzealous with my cleaning. Our house was spotless and his clothes always washed and ironed perfectly. If I was going to bother to do something, then I was going to do it well. I took care of our daughters and kept them involved in many extracurricular activities such as swim team, synchronized swimming, piano lessons (unlike my father, I was happy to pay for my children to take lessons), orchestra, and church.

I loved working on the hair of clients, friends, and family members in my basement shop where stimulating conversation was never lacking. My vegetable garden and my rose garden were luscious and thriving, and I enjoyed all my volunteering at church and in the community. Being busy every day and accomplishing many things that I wanted to do made me feel content, and I was happy.

Even though a majority of our money went back into the business, Walter was still generous with the money he spent on the girls and me. As I mentioned earlier, I made many of the girls' outfits as well as my own since my mother had taught me how to sew at a young age, but year after year Walter still insisted on getting us nice, new things. There were also yearly trips to the beach in Wildwood, New Jersey, and times when he would take us out to dinner so that I didn't have to cook or clean up. I have fond memories of enjoying crab cakes at fancy restaurants while Judy and Dee-Dee sipped Shirley Temples laden with dark red cherries. Judy would get so excited to go to Beck's restaurant for their snapper soup that her eyes would glow with anticipation while I put on my favorite crimson lipstick. I was blessed far more than I deserved, and I knew it. My prideful self tinkered with the idea that all my hard work had finally paid off, but my humble self quickly recognized that life isn't fair, and it was neither I, nor fate, nor coincidence that had gotten me to where I was. It was God alone.

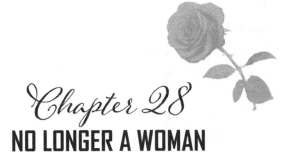

Chapter 28
NO LONGER A WOMAN

When our girls were still quite young, Walter and I were excited to find out that I was pregnant again. I pictured another miraculous little one in my arms. Would we finally have a boy? If it was another girl, that would be fun too. I could sew adorable matching dresses for all three of the girls to wear to church. We already had girl clothes, shoes, and toys so wouldn't need to purchase anything brand new unless we wanted something different. Our house had three bedrooms, so I mulled over keeping Dee-Dee and Judy together and giving the new baby the third room, which was now my sewing room. After waiting three months and visiting my gynecologist twice, I started telling all my family and friends the exciting news.

In hindsight, I recognize that I took many things for granted when it came to my third pregnancy. I just assumed that everything would be fine. Our baby would be born healthy without any complications, and our family would grow to five. I distinctly remember the morning when I once again learned the egregious lesson that just because I planned out exactly how I wanted my life to be didn't mean that this world would comply. I was sitting on the toilet in the downstairs half bath looking up to read the colorful plaque that I'd hung on the wall facing me.

For what seemed like the thousandth time, I smiled and giggled to myself about the words written there: "If you sprinkle when you tinkle, be a sweetie and wipe the seatie." Walter always said that I was easily amused; apparently, he was right because soon I was guffawing loud enough to bring him knocking on the bathroom door asking me what was so funny. It wasn't until I wiped myself that I noticed blood on the toilet paper. It wasn't a lot but enough to concern me because I'd never bled through any of my other pregnancies. I attempted to be calm while I called my doctor and made an appointment to go into his office later in the week.

Eagerly and anxiously I waited to be called back into the examination room. Once there, the nurse weighed me, took my temperature, and checked my blood pressure. I waited for another twenty-five minutes until the doctor finally came into the sterile room. He put the Pinard horn below my belly bottom and proceeded to slowly move it all around. As soon as I looked at his grave face, I knew. "I'm sorry," he said. "I cannot find the baby's heartbeat."

"Please try again!" I begged. He did and then let me listen for myself. I heard only the horribly deafening sound of soundlessness instead of the strong heartbeat that I'd discerned on my previous visit. The next thing I knew, I was having an uncomfortable pelvic exam.

"I'm sorry," the doctor repeated. "Your baby is dead." He handed me some tissues and went to get a nurse. I sat there in shock. A few confused tears tumbled down my cheeks. I heard something about scraping out the contents of my uterus or else letting my body do it naturally. Then somebody let me go out the back door so that I wouldn't have to walk through the crowded waiting room full of expectant mothers. I sat down in my car, laid my head on top of my arms that crisscrossed the hot steering wheel, and wept. "Why did this happen God? Why?"

As soon as I got home, I immediately called Walter. It must have been difficult for him to decipher my blubbering as he tried to understand why his wife who never cried aloud was sobbing. I didn't ask him to, but he immediately got into his car and drove back to Philadelphia. I had no words, so he just let me cry on his chest. His blue-gray eyes looked so sad when I finally lifted my head to look into them. Would our baby have had his hazel eyes? I'd have liked that.

It was completely alien for me to appear weak or fragile, and I hated the fact that I was breaking down in this pitiful way. I had to pull myself together immediately. It was Friday, and the next day was the Saturday that I was scheduled to host a baby shower for a neighbor and friend who lived three houses down. As soon as I told her of my loss, she said that she would understand if I wanted to cancel the party. I refused. My pain shouldn't ruin her special day. I told her that it would make me feel better to see her happy and that being busy with her party would focus my mind on good things. Even so, hosting that baby shower at my house the day after I found out that I had lost my own baby was one of the hardest things I've ever had to do. I was smothered by everything *baby*. The blue and pink decorations, tiny infant clothes, and shiny toys were everywhere I looked. I was drowning in a sea of eager, jubilant faces extolling the deliciousness of my rich finger foods and white icing cake with its turquoise lettering—*Congratulations on Your Baby!* As every conversation revolved about pregnancy and babies, there was no other topic of discussion for me to eagerly join. I foolishly daydreamed for a moment and saw my baby's chubby, cherub cheeks and big doe eyes. *Stop it!* I screamed at myself inside my head. *Just stop it!* I returned to reality by forcing myself to remember that this day was about my friend, not me, and that it needed to be that way. I wouldn't let myself think about anything other than that until the baby shower was over.

My personal decision was not to go to the antiseptic hospital but to leave my body alone to take care of itself. For weeks, I was disturbed to see blood every time I used the bathroom. My regret was palpable and I doubted myself. It made me wonder if maybe I should have had the D&C and gotten everything over with more quickly. But then again, it wasn't as if I was going to forget that I'd lost our baby just because I no longer saw blood. There was no denying it. I knew that I would never cease to remember this death, but I was hopeful that with the passing of time would come an easing of my suffering.

Poor Walter. When he married me, he took on all the heavy baggage that I brought with me from my childhood. I was not always easy to deal with even before the loss of our child, and now the pain and stress of it was definitely putting a strain on our marriage. We dealt with it differently, and I felt like my way was the only and best way. Walter was so supportive at first, but then I got very angry at him for what I perceived as him moving on too quickly. He never wanted to talk about our baby and clearly didn't understand that I was still very much in pain even though he seemed to be completely over it. I was haunted with thoughts—*This is the day my baby would have been born*; *he would be a month old today; he would be walking by now*; and so on. It frustrated me that I couldn't picture my child in my mind because I didn't know hair color, eye color, or shape of face. How dare Walter question me about how long I was going to keep thinking about our child? I wanted to spring at him and claw his eyes out when he asked me that. How could he be so mean? He was lucky that all I did was say that I felt like he wasn't supporting me, and that he didn't understand what I was going through. Of course he didn't. How could he really fully understand? Our baby had not been growing inside of him. He had never heard the heartbeat and then not heard it. It took time, but we both had to learn to let each other grieve in our own way and to communicate our feelings and needs to one other. Supporting each other didn't necessarily mean that we agreed; it meant that we chose to love one other even when we didn't feel as if we liked each other much at all.

Sadness turned into acceptance after much time passed. I came to strongly feel in my heart that there had been something physically wrong with my baby—very wrong—and that he or she would have had a very painful and difficult life constantly struggling to survive. I wouldn't have chosen for my child to die, but God knew that I would never have been able to stand seeing my child suffer. It might truly have been too much for me. Would I have let it destroy my marriage, my other children, my faith in God? Until the day when we are reunited, I can only rest in the knowledge that my baby is with my Lord experiencing unimaginable love and peace.

Soon after my miscarriage, my gynecologist strongly advised me not to have any more pregnancies. He said that the baby would never survive because my uterus would never sustain and hold him or her and that I would likely die myself if I tried. It was not the news that I wanted to hear. I never liked being told what to do without being given any choices. I once again felt like that exhausted, overworked child on the farm. Here was another man crushing my dreams, and I just had to take it. It burned me up inside to feel so powerless.

During that time, my sisters were a great help in consoling me emotionally, and their prayers lifted my spirits, but physically, I was still plagued with bleeding that almost never seemed to stop. For a year and a half after my miscarriage, I continued to bleed. The doctor told me that my only option was to have a complete hysterectomy. Once again, I didn't feel that I really had any choice. I thought of my mother and of her long and painfully drawn out death at an early age. I didn't want to keep bleeding, and I didn't want to die and leave my girls motherless; so even though I was only in my late thirties, I went through with the hysterectomy. I felt tremendous grief and depression over losing my fertility and several of my female body parts. I felt like I had been robbed of my womanhood and actually and figuratively felt empty. It was both a physically and emotionally painful six weeks of recovery before I finally started to feel like myself again.

One night, just a few months later, I awoke in my bed to wet sheets that were wringing with sweat. "It is so hot in here," I moaned to Walter before jumping out of bed to throw open the windows in the dead of winter. I soon learned that my hysterectomy had catapulted my body into stronger than normal symptoms of very early menopause. It seemed like I had just exchanged one problem for another. "Please tell me that you are kidding," I remember saying to the doctor. He tried to appease me, but to no avail. All he got for his troubles was a very unladylike utterance of "Dammit!" as I stormed back down the hall towards the exit.

My acute irritability and anxiety brought on by my early menopause were both vexing and embarrassing to me and to my family. Judy took it in stride, but I know that I drove Walter and Dee crazy while I went through this unwelcome stage of life. I understood just how awful I was when I saw the sheer mortification and embarrassment on Dee's face one weekend afternoon when our family was walking down the boardwalk in Wildwood. I was ranting loudly about someone or something I wasn't happy with, and everyone around us was staring at me. Dee's face was red, and her large, brown eyes stayed focused intently on the ground. In that moment, I knew her extreme discomfort was because of me and completely my fault.

My mood swings were terrible, and I felt irritated and uneasy all the time. It was so difficult to keep from exploding at any little thing, and I found it even more difficult than usual to keep my anger and lack of patience contained. Looking back, my hormones were out of control; therefore, my anxiety was at its highest level ever. I believe that a medication to calm my emotions would have helped me tremendously, but I didn't ask for it, nor did anyone suggest it because things like that weren't talked about back then. I was lucky to come through that ordeal with my family still intact because I know that I was difficult to be around, although I tried hard not to be so . . . well . . . schlecht. I said many prayers and yelled out "God, please help me" daily, and in retrospect, I am sure that similar words and prayers were uttered by my husband and children because they had to live with me. We all survived, thankfully, and there even came a time when I could look back at that particular struggle as the figurative thorn in my side that kept me humble and relying on God instead of my very humanly flawed self.

Chapter 29

MY NON-GLAMOROUS BUT GLORIOUS LIFE

Continuing on with my normal daily life, after losing my baby and my womanhood, felt less awkward and forced as more and more time passed. I once again enjoyed driving myself back and forth to church functions several times a week. I thought nothing of the fact that others considered it odd for a woman to be driving herself anywhere, especially to activities that didn't involve grocery shopping or getting her hair done at the hairdresser. My friend and neighbor Eleanor thanked me one day for picking her up to attend Bible study and commented that she admired my ability to drive myself wherever I wanted to go. I warmly encouraged her to do the same. She had a license but hadn't driven anywhere in ten years out of fear and a complete, complacent reliance on her husband. I supported her efforts to practice driving and accompanied her on many an outing until she felt comfortable enough to drive on her own.

It was no big deal to me, but Eleanor said that I was an inspiration to her. "You are strong and independent but still godly," she expressed cheerfully. I laughed aloud because the word *godly* was not one I would have chosen to describe myself. I was loud, assertive, opinionated, and bossy. If I didn't think something was right or felt like somebody was mistreating me or another person, I would not back down, but instead would become an unrelenting force of fury made all the more powerful by my personal perspective of righteousness.

"Godly Eleanor?" I scoffed. "I don't know about that! I can relate really well to Jesus when he angrily chased the people out of the temple for making his 'Father's house into a den of thieves,' but I need to conscientiously and consistently remind myself of the Jesus who remained mostly silent except for uttering the words 'I am' to Pilate after being beaten, mocked, and whipped."

Eleanor smiled and parted her lips as if to speak but then didn't.

"Eleanor, you and I both know that I can never keep my big mouth shut," I added emphatically.

Before I could further decline her accolade and deflect her praise, Eleanor cut me off by adding, "Wanda, you are always very humble, not fully appreciating your own worth, so just be quiet and accept the compliment."

"Well, I guess I had better just say 'thank you' and not fight you on this one Eleanor," I answered before giving her a quick wink. Fifty years later, and over twenty years after her husband had passed away, Eleanor still reminisced about how much more self-sufficient and strong she became after I got her driving. It was quite powerful to recognize how something that I perceived as such a meager gesture was truly a life-changing experience for someone else.

I always loved sharing vegetables and flowers from my gardens with friends, neighbors, and family members. Hearing their comments about my *green thumb* made me feel proud about having farming in my blood. People often made special requests for my homemade bread, butter pickles, dill pickles, and pickled watermelon rind, and I was happy to oblige as long as I had plenty left for Walter. Whatever I made was always the first to sell out at the church bazaars, and people unabashedly ran to the table where I set up the goodies I'd prepared. I also enjoyed being involved in the Home Extension Services of Pennsylvania and was very active with my local group. I attended all of the meetings and then spent a great deal of time putting things I'd learned into practice when gardening, sewing, or making all sorts of creative, artsy things. One of my favorite projects was creating decoupage picture frames (which quickly lined the wall opposite the stair rail leading to our second floor) before I moved on to another enterprise. Constantly learning invigorated me and made me feel like I was catching up on things that I'd been deprived of while under the dictatorship of my father.

Helping others while doing my normal, everyday activities became a natural way of serving God, and I was surprised to discover that it filled me with delight and peace. Less *me* and more *them* made me happier, which was completely ironic considering how as a child I hated when carloads of people swarmed our farm forcing me to become a begrudging hostess. My mother, if she had still been alive, would have been shocked to see me frequently inviting people over to my home. It was the Belinsky house that all the cousins would come to for sledding. Down the glittering, white hills of the golf course across the street, the kids would fly away the winter days. After hours of happy squeals, contagious laughter, and occasional peals of terror, the frozen children would enter my kitchen and dining room with faces of eager anticipation looking forward to my homemade hot chocolate and scrumptious spritz sugar cookies.

At Christmas time, I made hundreds of those sugar cookies. They would be spread out everywhere for Judy and Dee-Dee to help me cover with red hots and sugars of various colors. As soon as I pulled out my aluminum Mirro Cooky Press, the girls couldn't wait to select the different plates or tips to insert and start decorating. Their big eyes would glisten with anticipation as they watched the cookie dough transform into Christmas trees, wreaths, camels, snowflakes, and stars.

When my girls were in middle school, I decided to have dances down in our basement. All my nieces and nephews would be invited to come over for dance lessons followed by Aunt Wanda's refreshments. I wanted somewhere safe for the kids to mingle and to enjoy themselves. Their young laughter reminded me of all the fun I'd had with my church youth group when I was a child. Beautiful memories of precious times flooded back. They were times when I was able to escape the exhausting, physical labor forced on me by my father. I hoped that such remembrances would stay with me and never be forgotten. They represented so much joy and laughter that my father never would have condoned had he known; and yet, Father was completely responsible for providing those opportunities since he was the one who introduced us to church. It was situational irony at its best and undoubtedly God's plan all along.

Walter and I also enjoyed taking dance lessons together. We did the Fox Trot, Rumba, Mambo, Waltz, and Salsa and laughed at ourselves a lot along the way. These in turn were the dances that I taught the kids in our basement. They would do them together and then always end with a time of free dancing to music of their choice from their favorite radio stations. I'd make the children punch and let them gorge themselves on my chocolate chip or spritz cookies and salty snacks. Sometimes the adults played Pinochle upstairs while the kids danced, and other times they simply submerged themselves in conversations filled with thrilling stories and obvious hyperbole. I imagine that God was up there in heaven laughing to himself at the complete 180 degree change that had happened in my heart. Instead of loathing company, I loved having people all around me! It really was an unexpected miracle.

Chapter 30
LOVE THY NEIGHBOR

Once I was married and had children, I really felt like I was mature and an excellent reader of people. For example, I allowed my daughters to befriend the Fabers, our wonderful next-door neighbors, and that was a fantastic decision. But I also proved myself gullible and naïve when I permitted another neighbor to penetrate my inner circle. Being optimistic is a good thing, but unfortunately, it may only take one deceitful person to obliterate your trust and positivity, turning you into a cynic.

Since first moving to Leon Street, I had always been friendly with all of my neighbors and enjoyed conversing with them. Since we had a corner lot, there wasn't a house directly on our right, but we did have neighbors to our left. Soon after Walter and I moved into our house, Poppy and Kee-Kee Faber moved in next door. They were quite a bit older than we were but had no children of their own. Pop was a talented artist who had retired by the time they lived beside us, so the Fabers were always at home. They took an immediate liking to me, and I greatly enjoyed them too since I sometimes felt lonely due to all the hours that Walter worked. Talking with them was easy, and we quickly grew close. When the girls were born, the Fabers fawned all over them exclaiming that they were the most beautiful, precious children they'd ever seen. It was only natural that my girls would grow up thinking of Poppy and Kee-Kee as surrogate grandparents since they showered so much attention and love on them. Because the Fabers had no children or grandchildren of their own, my girls were their hearts.

The grandparent-like bond between my girls and the Fabers was made stronger by the fact that all Judy and Dee-Dee knew of my own father was that he was an unsmiling presence at family gatherings on the farm. All the grandkids would begrudgingly stop their playing to line up and walk one by one to Grandfather Konschak's chair in order to kiss his scratchy cheek. Dee-Dee complained that he stunk of cigars and made gagging sounds when she saw him spitting putrid tobacco juice into the metal spittoon next to his chair.

"That is so disgusting," she would wail.

"Just be thankful that you don't have to clean the spittoon out," I'd answer.

The fourteen grandchildren couldn't wait to be done with this forced tradition. Afterwards, they sped back to their games and laughter far away from their stern and intimidating grandfather, who rarely interacted with them. I used to laugh to myself to see the dramatic changes in the kids' faces. Their countenances went from serious to joyful once they were able to escape him and go back to their playing. Knowing that they wouldn't have to kiss Grandfather again until the next family gathering was a goliath relief. I noticed that my girls, as well as several of their cousins, immediately wiped their lips against their shirtsleeves after kissing my father, and I got a kick out of that too.

Alma never even bothered herself with knowing any of her husband's grandchildren's names! Can you believe that? What a sin! She was their grandmother by marriage and also their great-aunt by blood, but she had no interest in any one of them.

Whether her ignoring of the fourteen Konschak grandchildren was carelessness or ostentatious contempt, I don't know. It was sad though, really sad.

On the other side of our family were Walter's parents. They hadn't been a part of our girls' lives right away because of their grudge against Walter for marrying me. Once my in-laws had finally accepted Walter back into their family, I know that Judy and Dee were truly blessed and happy to be able to get to know them. Still, even though John and Mary Belinsky did eventually accept and love Judy and Dee-Dee, it seemed to me that my girls somehow sensed the earlier rejection and resulting pain and were never as close to their grandparents as they could have been. It was unfortunate, too, that the opportunities to actually see their grandparents were few and mainly revolved around me inviting John and Mary to dinner at our house.

All of these family circumstances led to a very meaningful and beautiful relationship between Poppy and Kee-Kee and their *adopted* granddaughters, Judy and Dee-Dee. One or both of the girls would wander next door almost daily to sit on beloved Poppy's stool and talk incessantly to him while he worked on paintings in his workshop. He was extremely gifted, and many of his beautiful paintings ended up in the hands of two smiling, pretty little girls whom he loved. My daughters also couldn't wait to be spoiled and doted on by Kee-Kee. She really was an expert when it came to spoiling them rotten and at the same time was very protective of both Judy and Dee-Dee when they were little.

The only times that Kee-Kee and I didn't get along were when she got angry with me for getting out my little horse whip and using it for discipline. She also hated it when I spanked the girls. I did have high expectations and was strict with my children, but it was for their own good. Kee-Kee wouldn't talk to me for days after she witnessed me spanking them or heard about it when one of the girls would run over to her house afterwards with tears raining down her blotchy cheeks. Their little downcast faces and the red handprint on their bottoms or legs always infuriated Kee-Kee who believed I was much too hard on my girls. If she had only known what I had been through as a child, she may have seen things differently. She'd soothe them with cold soda pop, hard candies, and little trinkets or gifts and then go on to entertain them in her garden or house. Dee's favorite comforting gift from Kee-Kee was a purple, padded box full of personal handkerchiefs, many of which had the letter K delicately embroidered on them. I guess Kee-Kee felt that the unique and colorful handkerchiefs, all beautiful in their own way, would bring Dee-Dee comfort the next time she had a need to dry her big, brown eyes. One day in the distant future, Dee would pass this very same box of treasured handkerchiefs on to her oldest daughter, Kathi.

Whenever Kee-Kee angrily refused to talk to me because I'd punished my children, I'd just leave her alone since I knew that we were never going to agree on how to discipline, and besides, the girls loved her so. After a few days of ignoring each other, she would come back around to her warm self, and we would laugh and talk in the backyard while I worked in my garden or amongst my roses and other flowers. Poppy and Kee-Kee were good neighbors who I was thankful for, so I wasn't prepared to encounter a neighbor who was not good.

Two houses down from us, in a very large and impressive home, there lived a highly attractive couple. He was the rich owner of an insurance agency. She was the organ player at their church, and they were known to be very pious and devoted Baptists. He was older but recognizably handsome and obviously well-off when it came to finances. He never seemed to be at his office, instead choosing to be at home throughout the week while his employees made him money. He was very friendly and personable and often stopped by to talk. I enjoyed his copious compliments about my physical appearance and was amused by our carefree banter. He had a newer model, expensive camera and took many pictures of both the girls and me. He always gave the photographs to me once they were developed, and they were quite impressive. I thought nothing of it at first, believing that he was only a kind, generous man.

Once he found out that I was a beautician, he started making appointments with me to give him manicures. I eventually started to feel uncomfortable because he was always wanting to give me hugs or linger with his hand on my shoulder. After a few months of giving him manicures, he started trying to put his free hand on my arm while I worked and then even tried to hold my hand. I ignored it by simply brushing his hand aside and tried to finish as quickly as possible. I suddenly understood why he never made his appointments with me while Walter was at home but always chose weekdays while my husband was at work. After the day that he tried to grasp my hand, I wouldn't make any appointments with him unless I could have Judy or Dee-Dee downstairs in the basement with me. Their innocent, little eyes watching seemed to convince him that any foolhardy, inappropriate gestures would be relayed to their father once he returned from work. This new arrangement worked out well for several peaceful weeks until my neighbor dared to slide his hand under the table and onto my bare knee, attempting to leave it there while Dee-Dee skipped happily around us. I slapped his hand away and gave him a fierce and deadly look that didn't require words. He smiled seductively and gently placed the money he owed me onto the table before walking up the basement stairs and showing himself out. I didn't know what to do. Was I blowing things out of proportion? Should I tell his faithful, unsuspecting wife and my husband or stay silent avoiding drama? It was a dilemma that didn't appear to have a clear-cut answer. Before I had made up my mind on a course of action, I found myself cornered. Just a few days later while the girls were still at school, I heard the clicking sound of a doorknob turning behind me. I was in my kitchen taking lamb out of the refrigerator for dinner when he walked in uninvited through the back door. He knew that I kept it unlocked during the day since it was the closest access to my garden.

"What are you doing in here?" I bellowed. "You need to leave right now!"

"I just came to make another appointment for a manicure," he offered.

"There will be no more manicures for you," I stated firmly.

"But Wanda," he whispered as he moved towards me reaching out his arms.

Before I knew it, he was groping my breasts. I jerked back slapping his arms away from me. I was furious but rational enough to recognize my dilemma. We were alone in my house with all the windows and doors closed since it was a cool enough fall day to require keeping heat inside the house. He was bigger than me and both taller and stronger. His tremendous hand could cover my entire face like a candle snuffer over a vivid, orange flame. My screams would never be heard. What he didn't count on was that I was Schlechta Wanda Konschak who had been fighting all her life. I would be the hot wax that would burn him even when he seemed to have carefully planned everything out. When he reached for me again, I slammed my fist into his unsuspecting face with all the adrenaline that I had inside me. Bam! If he had been armed, I would have suffered for my brazen response, but he wasn't, and he was fully unprepared for the wrath that I was unleashing on him. He stumbled back, his hands gesturing upwards towards his bleeding face where I had purposely punched him with my left hand. (It seemed fitting to have my engagement and wedding rings serve as weapons.) Before he could recover, I kicked him as hard as I could in the groin. It seemed like I could see the whites of his eyes as he crumbled onto the floor groaning.

"Now get out! And if you ever do anything like this to me or anyone else again, you will live to regret it because I will expose you to the whole world and ruin you!" I screamed while seizing an oversized, shiny butcher knife off of my cutting board and holding it high above my head. I dared not move while he slowly pulled himself off of the ground by grabbing the freezer door handle. He looked like a stealthy beetle preparing for flight. His baleful eyes stayed fixed on me as he limped sideways towards the back door and exited. Then he was gone, trying to walk as nonchalantly as possible through my backyard to the sidewalk and towards his house, grimacing all the while. How he explained his wounded condition to his wife, I don't know, but I do know that he once again started going to his office every weekday morning and staying all day long. Sometimes his friendly wife would catch sight of me outside and wave happily. Was that a meek look of thanks that I saw in her eyes? It appeared to me like she had given her husband a none-too-pleasant ultimatum and that his wholehearted acquiescence had saved him. I wanted to believe that he had changed, but my cynicism was engorged with memories of how he had once appeared so charming and friendly on the outside while harboring a lying, deceitful snake on the inside. I was never again so trusting of people, and it was hard for me to determine whether this newest loss of my innocence was a beneficial or a terrible thing.

Chapter 31

WONDERFULLY GOOD AT BEING BEAUTIFULLY BAD

I was thankful for all that I had in my adult life: a loving husband with a successful business, a beauty shop in my basement, my children, my church, my garden, my roses, and most importantly the knowledge of God's grace and provision. Would things always be delightful? Easy? Of course not! But if I could hold tightly to my faith, I knew that I could and would survive the ugly, painful times and once again have happiness and peace, if not in this world, then in the next. I was eventually able to look back at many of the traumatic events of my life and see how my all-powerful God had brought some good out of the most terrible situations, which was no small task. If my father hadn't picked Alma over me, would I have ever left the farm and gone to beauty school? Without being a hairdresser, what were the chances that I would have ever met Irene and, consequently, Walter? If Walter hadn't almost died from TB, would his parents ever have accepted him back and welcomed our children? These were questions that I felt I knew the answer to, but there were other anguishes that I had yet to understand. I planned to ask God about those once I got to heaven. If there was one thing I knew, it was that it was impossible for me to grasp everything that had happened to me in my life with complete comprehension. That is where my faith came in to quiet my turmoil.

One Saturday afternoon, I went to visit a dear friend of mine who had stopped coming to church. I handed her the aromatic meal I'd prepared for her dinner, and then we sat down to talk. She smiled slightly and asked me if I thought she was a terrible person now that she'd been skipping church and avoiding phone calls from our pastor. I laughed and answered, "Well, a very wise minister told me once that a sin is a sin is a sin, and I shouldn't ever think that anyone else's sin is any greater than my own." My response seemed to relieve some of her tension and give her the courage to ask me the real question that was on her mind.

"How can a loving God allow horrible things to happen?" she blurted out with anger in her eyes. I knew immediately that she was specifically referring to the sexual abuse of her son at the hands of one of her oldest family friends. The man was now in prison for his crimes, but her son continued to suffer from depression. Six months had passed since her son had attempted suicide by purposely driving his mother's car at full speed through a barricade and into the icy Delaware River. She had been the one to discover her beloved, only son's suicide note expressing how he had felt hopeless and unable to cope with his trauma. He hadn't died but was seriously injured suffering severe lacerations to his face and permanent damage to both his legs. My friend was left with a twenty-year-old disfigured son who would have to use a walker for the rest of his life.

I most certainly did not have all the answers for her broken heart, but I knew that I wanted to share my honest beliefs without sounding too preachy or long winded. In that split second before I answered, I worried about offending her or making her angry with me. Without speaking aloud, I asked myself, *When you see someone you love about to get seriously hurt, don't you reach out to help, even if it means possibly facing personal, painful consequences yourself? Of course I do,* I yelled back. She had no idea that I was having a whole conversation with myself in my head.

I looked directly into her questioning eyes and asked, "What kind of a friend would I be if I was standing right beside you and didn't try to help when you needed me because I was too scared of making you mad?"

She looked at me with a strained and inquiring glance before answering, "You'd be a selfish and terrible friend if you didn't try to help me no matter the consequences to yourself."

"Yes, I agree that I would be a really terrible friend," I responded adamantly. "I am not going to be a schlecht friend! Even at the risk of offending you and losing our friendship, I am determined to speak my mind about my faith in Jesus."

I leaned forward in my chair and silently prayed that she'd be receptive. I told her that I knew for sure that God never intended for evil to be in our world. He created us with free will. We were never meant to be puppets on a string. We all have always been free to choose; unfortunately, all the way back to Adam and Eve, people have chosen to do evil.

"God could have decided to leave us to our own destruction and damnation in this broken world, but he had mercy," I calmly stated.

"How did he show mercy?" She scoffed.

"Well, once we all chose sin, it became impossible for us to be in the presence of the perfect God. There was only one way for us to be redeemed. Someone who had never sinned had to take our sin and stand between us and God, so that when God looked at us, he would only see the sinless Savior." I smiled. "That way was Jesus."

"So this grace stuff we hear about in church all the time is because of Jesus?" she asked in a way that sounded more like a statement than a question.

"Yes. Yes." I repeated, feeling as if a weight had been lifted off my heart.

I truly did understand her anger with God. I had been there myself and only hoped that she would allow God to love and heal her with the peace that only he can give. For my part, the only other things that I could do that day were to say how very sorry I was for the devastating things that had happened to her and to hold her gently while she sobbed on my shoulder. I told myself that her tragedy would be one of the first things I asked God about when I met him face to face. I read my Bible for an extra long time that night before saying my prayers, pulling the soft blanket up to my cheek, and falling into a much needed sleep.

My conversation with my friend got me thinking quite deeply about my own issues. I wanted to condemn my father for making my childhood and that of my siblings one of traumatizing servitude. I wanted to blame him for the loss of the most important person in my life, my mother. I needed him to hold himself accountable and to say he was sorry for his cruelty, coldness, violence, greed, selfishness, and especially for reminding me mercilessly that I was bad. I fiercely hated him for making me believe that I was indeed schlecht. Even before my very wise daughters started telling me that I needed to forgive my father, I already knew that I needed to do just that. But I simply couldn't, not yet. It infuriated me that he never once took responsibility and said he was sorry. I argued with God about it in a continuous discourse: "Why should I have to forgive my father when he has never repented or even admitted he was wrong? I know you have forgiven me, but it's still not fair! It's too hard!" I was an adult, but I knew that I sounded like a child. Even before my father died, I felt like God was telling me and showing me that forgiveness wasn't for my father but for myself and my relationship with God, but I still couldn't do it. That was a big mistake.

As the years passed by, my anger at my father festered and grew until I was remembering less and less of the good things from my past and was consumed and tortured by a fixation on the bad things from my childhood. I am sure that the Devil reveled in the pain I caused myself year after year. I knew that I should show grace and forgive and finally purge myself from the pain, but that would mean that I had to release my excruciatingly tight grip on the source of my anger, which was neither a natural nor an easy thing for me to do. The longer I stubbornly held on, the harder forgiveness became. I am thankful for the patience of my God. For those of you who love me and wonder, I can only say that any forgiveness that occurred is fully known only by God and me and is not to be revealed on this side of heaven.

One thing that I can tell you, however, with absolute conviction and complete assurance is that I have always been and continue to be wonderfully good at being beautifully bad Wanda! I understand now that being bad is good when it ultimately leads you to a life of faith and purpose. There is a beautiful blessing to be found in the battle and a wondrous reward at the end. With this statement, my story is complete. I'd like to leave you with one of my granddaughter's favorite poems. Kathi says that it reminds her of me, and I have enjoyed it very much as a nourisher of my soul and a light in dark times. May it and my true story encourage and empower you.

Love,

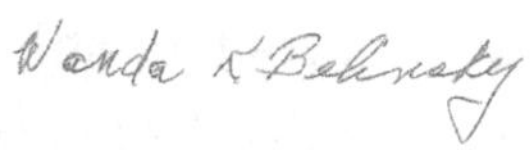

Music

by Ralph Waldo Emerson

Let me go where'er I will,
I hear a sky-born music still:
It sounds from all things old,
It sounds from all things young,
From all that's fair, from all that's foul,
Peals out a cheerful song.

It is not only in the rose,
It is not only in the bird,
Not only where the rainbow glows,
Nor in the song of woman heard,
But in the darkest, meanest things
There alway, alway something sings.

Tis not in the high stars alone,
Nor in the cup of budding flowers,
Nor in the redbreast's mellow tones,
Nor in the bow that smiles in showers,
But in the mud and scum of things
There alway, alway something sings.

EPILOGUE

Wanda's love for her Christian faith and for education can be seen in that both Judy and Dee went to Concordia College in Chicago to become teachers. Judy then married Paul, a Lutheran pastor, and moved to Michigan. They have three sons as well as a daughter and ten grandchildren. Three of Judy's four children are teachers. Dee and her husband Jim were both Lutheran school teachers in St. Louis, Missouri, and then in Deerfield Beach, Florida. Dee would go on to create a developmental preschool program at Zion Lutheran Church and School and served as the director there for many years before becoming the director of a Methodist preschool in Columbia, South Carolina. She eventually returned to her first love, teaching. Jim was a teacher for more than twenty-five years before going to Lutheran Theological Southern Seminary in Columbia, South Carolina, to become a minister. He has spent the last twenty-one years as a pastor in South Carolina. Jim and Dee have three daughters and six granddaughters. Their eldest daughter, Kathi, who is the author of this book, is also a teacher. Kathi was blessed with many years of personally enjoying her grandmother's animated stories about her life as Schlecht Wanda. Those treasured conversations along with recordings

Wanda made before her death, letters, family reunion materials, online research, and interviews with remaining family members have enabled the writing of this novel.

Walter retired from Bel-Far Steel Company in 1975, and he and Wanda enjoyed traveling to Europe and all around the United States together before his death at the age of eighty-one. They had fun bowling, walking, and doing lawn work together. They also especially treasured spending time with their seven grandchildren: Kathi, Jeanene, Jodi, Bill, Philip, Andrew, and Jennifer.

Wanda lived in the house she and Walter built on Leon Street in Philadelphia until she was in her eighties. She kept herself busy with her church activities and volunteerism and continued to maintain her vegetable garden and stunningly beautiful and fragrant rose garden. Wanda stayed healthy by swimming laps at the YMCA several mornings a week. She could easily be spotted as the attractive lady who always wore a swimming cap to protect her hair and who never ever put her face in the water. Wanda eventually went to live with Dee and Jim. She would later split her time between Dee in South Carolina and Judy in Michigan. To the joy and occasional vexation of her family, Wanda was lively, opinionated, and feisty until her death in 2010 at the age of ninety-four.

The Konschak farmhouse still stands in Hartly, Delaware. It was beautifully maintained and lived in by Susanne Konschak until her death on April 30, 2019. Most of the Konschak land has been sold and is now covered with houses and neighborhoods. A hint of the area's past can be seen on a street sign labeling one of the roads as Konschak Avenue. The work ethic, compassion, and strength of character Wanda possessed continue to be passed on through the generations of her family still living in that area and beyond.

Saint John's Lutheran Church (which John Konschak helped found in 1923) also still stands at 113 Lotus Street and remains active to this day ninety-six years later. Saint John's even has daughter congregations that started as mission churches. They include Concordia Lutheran Church in Wilmington, Delaware; Christ Lutheran in Seaford, Delaware; Peace Lutheran Church in Smyrna, Delaware; and Trinity Lutheran Church in Chestertown, Maryland.

FAMILY TREE OF JOHN KONSCHAK

John Konschak b: 7 27 1879 in Lodz, Poland when the majority of the population was German d: 1955
+Pauline Zarbok b: 1 30 1881 in Olikof, Russia/Poland d: 1932
2nd wife Alma Z. d: 1987

• Gustav Konschak b: 4 14 1901 Lodz, Russia/Poland d: 6 1980
+ Matilda Berger b: 3 14 1905 in Leupolz, Germany d: 1999

• John Konschak Jr. b: 1902 Lodz d: 1938

• Otto Konschak b: 1903 in Millville, NJ d: 1908

• Julia Konschak b: 1905 in Philadelphia, PA d: 1988
+ Edmund Hintz b: 1900 d: 1943

Edward John Hintz b: 1931 +/- Mary Rowland + Carolyn Klotz b: 1943
Raymond Edward Hintz b: 1954 + Sue Mattson
Joseph Mattson (stepson)+ Jenny Brown
Kiley Grace Mattson b: 2001

Roy Allen Hintz b: 1955 d: 1988

Susan D. Hintz b: 1956 + Dennis Sutherlin in 1999
Christine Dawejko b: 1977
Edmund M. Dawejko b: 1979

From Edward's 2nd marriage:
John Edward Hintz b: 1968 + Marie
Heidi Marlene Hintz b: 1977 + Noel Hwang

Janice Elsie Hintz b: 6 1937 + John W. Harrington, Jr. b: 12 1937
John W. Harrington III b: 11 1962 + Maria Ritchie b: 1967
Cale J. Harrington b: 1990
Kyndal Harrington b: 1993 + Curtis Tekell in 2017

Deborah Sue Harrington b: 10 1964 + Brian McFadden b: 1962
Michael Brian McFadden b: 1993
Jennifer Kate McFadden b: 1995
Daniel Paul McFadden b: 1996
Kayla Grace McFadden b: 1998
Laurel Hope McFadden b: 2000
Mary Joy McFadden b: 2004
Emma Faith McFadden b: 2006
John David McFadden b: 2009

Glen D. Harrington b: 7 1966 + Tara Talmadge b: 1964
Thomas James Harrington b: 6 1992
Jillian Catherine Harrington b: 7 1995

Elaine Jule Hintz b: 1943 +/- George Heineman b: 1942 + Charles L. Christian b: 1945
George David Heineman, Jr. b: 1964 + Judith Anne Schneider b: 1965
John Austin Heineman b: 1994

Jaclyn Anne Heineman b: 1997
Jeffrey George Heineman b: 2004

Cynthia (Cindy) Lynn Heineman b: 1966 + Daniel James Branch b: 1967
Daniel Joseph Branch b: 1997
Megan Lynn Branch b: 2007

• William Konschak b: 1907 in Philadelphia, PA d: 9 2003
+ Olga Guse b: 6 29 1913 d: 1 2002
Carol Gene Konschak Lohrmann b: 5 1945

Robert William Konschak b: 2 1947 + Rhae Ann Smith b: 1 1947
William Rhey Konschak b: 5 1971
Madelyn Rigney Konschak b: 1 1995

• Emma Konschak b: 1910 in Marydel, DE d: 1998
+ Albert Hintz b: 1903 d: 1989
Doris Betty Hintz b: 2 1931 + William John Wood, Jr. b: 1930 d: 1974 + 2nd husband James C. Wilkes, Sr. b: 1923 d: 1994
William Scott Wood b: 1952 + Debra Ann Neid b: 1952
Kathlene Ann Wood b: 1984 + Michael Taylor b: 1984
Mason Taylor b: 2019

• Pauline (Paula) Konschak b: 1912 Marydel, DE d: 11 2005
+ John Conrad Bergmann b: 1909 d: 1969
Paula A. Bergmann b: 1940 + Joseph Butler Sullivan b: 2 1944 d: 5 1997 raised 2 foster sisters Linda M. Chopik b: 1975
Michael W. Chopik b: 1996
and Dawn M. Chopik b: 1977 + Thomas Finn b: 1975

John E. Bergmann b: 1943 d: 10 2018 + Dorothy Ann Dutill b: 1949
Monica L. Bergmann b: 1975
Andrew J. Bergmann b: 1977

Lois C. Bergmann b: 1947 + John F. Fafara b: 1934
Caroline L. Fafara b: 1977 + Joshua Stein b: 1975
Padin L. Stein b: 2005
Adler J. Stein b: 4 2008
Gavin E. Stein b. 4 2008

John M. Fafara b: 1982 + Nina Steskal b:1987
Gianna Fafara b: 2018

• Richard Konschak b: 1 18 1913 in Marydel, DE d: 7 1968 + Agnes Catherine Hinger b: 1912 d: 1 2005
Robert Paul Konschak b: 1941 d: 5 2018 +/- Kirsten Johansen b: 1941 + Eileen Olsen
Suzanne Bendix Konschak b: 1964 + Robert Charles LoRusso b: 1964
Hannah Elizabeth Bendix LoRusso b: 2001
Tobi Christine Bendix LoRusso b: 2002
Robert Charles LoRusso Jr. b: 2004
Joshua Christopher LoRusso b: 2008

Alan Richard Konschak b: 1968 + Joanne Marie Rega b: 1969

Mark Paul Konschak b: 1972 + Jennifer Ann Goenner b: 1974
Gavin H. Konschak b: 2001
Madison Skylar Konschak b: 2004

Walter Konschak b: 2 1943 d: 10 2018 +/- Carole Krotz b: 1947
+ Suzanne P. Anderson-Konschak b: 1953
Kimberly (Kimmy) Ann Konschak b: 1969 + H.L. Buch b: 8 1965
Trevor Austin Buch b: 1992
Ashley Nicole Buch b: 1995

Connie Lynn Konschak b: 1970 + Michael Alexander Krepich Jr. b: 11 1967
Michael A. Krepich III b: 1999
Samantha Catherine Krepich b: 2000
Ryan Krepich b: 2007
Lily Krepich b: 2010

Kristen (Krissy) Marie Konschak b: 1972 + John Williams IV b: 6 1966
John Henry Williams V b: 1999
Jake Matthew Williams b: 2001

Carole Ann Konschak b: 5 1977 + Frank Baisden b: 6 1961
Christopher Baisden b: 2006
Natalie Baisden b: 2008

From Walter Konschak's 2nd marriage:
Patti Konschak b: 1993

Evelyn Konschak b: 12 1946 + Michael Paglaiccetti b: 10 1945
Michele Annette Paglaiccetti b: 1968 + Thomas Nicholas Lamelza b: 1963
Thomas Augustus Lamelza b: 1990
Connor Austin Lamelza b: 1996
Hunter A. Lamelza b: 2002
Branden M. Lamelza b: 2004

Stephanie Anne Paglaiccetti b: 1 1970 + David Wayne Rossi b: 10 1967
Nathan Wayne Rossi b: 1999
Zachery Benjamin Rossi b: 2001
Eli Rossi b: 2005

Carlene Marie Paglaiccetti b: 12 1971 + Matthew Mull b: 1 1973
Samantha Marie Mull b: 1997
Gabrielle Katherine Mull b: 2001
Alexandra Evelyn Mull b: 2004

Michael Anthony Paglaiccetti b: 9 1975 +Lisa Hahn b: 3 1976
Olivia Paglaiccetti b: 2009
Michael Charles Paglaiccetti b: 2013
Christina Lee Paglaiccetti b: 1980 + Heppner
Micah Stone Heppner b: 2009
Uriah River Heppner b: 2011

- Wanda Konschak b: 1 16 1916 in Marydel, DE d: 2010 + Walter Belinsky b: 3 26 1908 d: 1989

Judith (Judy) Lea Belinsky b: 6 1943 + Rev. Paul Wargo b: 4 1941
William Walter Wargo b: 4 1973 + Michelle Seoul b: 4 1973
Michael William Wargo b: 3 2002
Autumn Wargo b: 5 2007

Phillip Paul Wargo b: 2 1976 + Nicki Hurttgam b: 12 1976
Keecie (Takrise) Chandler Wargo b: 5 2008
Tai (Taiku) Chandler Wargo b: 5 2008

Andrew Allen Wargo b: 2 1978 + Kelly Marie b: 1978
Natalie Lyn Wargo b: 6 2005
Kendall Arlie Wargo b: 5 2010

Jennifer Joy Wargo b: 7 1982 + Dominic Arthur Capoferi b: 1975
Trevor Thomas Capoferi b: 8 2004
Drew Dominic Capoferi b: 11 2006
Owen Joseph Capoferi b: 11 2006
Justin Lee Capoferi b: 9 2012

Dierdre (Dee) Ann Belinsky b: 8 1944 + Rev. James K. Glander b. 4 1944
Kathryn (Kathi) Deanne Glander b: 3 14 1973 + Henry Pittman Stogner b: 3 1973
Lydia Rose Stogner b: 5 2003
Jessica (Jessi) Faith Stogner b: 12 2006

Jeanene Leanne Glander b: 24 11 1974 + Jorgen Waldermo b: 4 1967
Mikala Elisabeth Waldermo b: 4 2005
Madison Rebekah Waldermo b: 2 2007

Jodene (Jodi) Suzanne Glander b: 10 24 1976 + Mike Ernest Jones b: 1 1977
Hannah Kathryn Jones b: 6 2006
Bria Margaret Jones b: 11 2008

• Albert M. Konschak b: 10 21 1918 in Marydel d: 5 16 2001 + Susanne Lissy b: 5 29 1921 d: 4 29 2019
Linda Konschak b: 1942 + John H. (Jack) Conrad b: 1937 d: 8 2010
Jackie Helen Conrad b: 1978 + Josh Etzweiler b: 1973
Silver Kiana Etzweiler b: 2005

Nancy Konschak b: 9 17 1943 +/- Gerald Thierwechter b: 1942 + Roger Hazzard b: 1949

Jennifer Lynn Thierwechter b: 5 06 1970 + Christopher Rambo b: 5 08 1969
Sarah Mackenzie Rambo b: 1998
Lindsey Aston Rambo b: 2002

Marlene Konschak b: 10 16 1945 + Linden Lee Boyer, Jr. b: 2 13 1945
Marcy Lynne Boyer b: 1 18 1975 + Mike Gomez b: 11 25 1970
Kyle E. Gomez b: 4 17 2003

Linden Lee Boyer III b: 2 19 1978 + Alyssa K. Marvin b: 4 26 1981
Jessica Marie Boyer b: 7 23 2001
Emily N. Boyer b: 1 07 2003
Katie Chae Boyer b: 4 21 2007

• Martha Konschak b: 3 29 1920 in Marydel d: 5 18 2001 + Raymond (Ray) Karutz b: 1912 d: 12 16 2000
Eileen Martha Karutz b: 5 29 1946 +/- M. Bielec +/-Paul Hanson
Lorie Bielic b: 9 1973

ABOUT THE AUTHOR

Kathryn G. Stogner is the granddaughter of Wanda K. Belinsky. She takes on her grandmother's persona to write this nonfiction narrative that reads like a memoir. Kathi's firsthand memories of her grandmother's stories, along with letters, interviews, various documents, online research, and Wanda's own cassette recordings have all been utilized as corroborating material in the creation of *Beautifully Bad Wanda*. Kathi is a licensed English and AIG (K-12) teacher with a BA in English Education and an MA in English, and she was certified by the National Board of Professional Teaching Standards in 2002. What truly qualifies her to create this quenching story is a feisty resolve to share her grandmother's spiritually enriching and motivational story with a thirsty world that needs its hopeful message right now!

Kathi currently resides in North Carolina with her husband, daughters, and dogs.

CONTACT KATHI

Connect with Kathi for more information, to learn about bringing her to your live event, or to find out how to get a free *Beautifully Bad Wanda* teaching unit for use in your classroom.

- Website: beautifullybadwanda.com created by Danielle E. Randolph
- Facebook:facebook.com/Kathi-G-Stogner-100549157956286/
- Email: kathi.glanderstogner@gmail.com
- Instagram: kathigstogner
- LinkedIn: linkedin.com/in/kathi-stogner-531184185

CPSIA information can be obtained
at www.ICGtesting.com
Printed in the USA
FSHW012232041119
63749FS

9 781545 661475